D1707526

# Memories
## of MAYBERRY

# Andy Griffith–from Cradle to College

Montage photos courtesy of Emmett Forrest and The Andy Griffith Museum, Mount Airy Visitors Information Center. Thanks to Robert Merritt for reproduction of the original photos.

*To Dennis*

*Enjoy!*

# Memories
## of MAYBERRY

**A NOSTALGIC
LOOK AT
*Andy Griffith's*
HOMETOWN:
MOUNT AIRY,
NORTH CAROLINA**

*Jewell M. Kutzer*
Jewell Mitchell Kutzer

Ɖ

Dynamic Living Press
St. Augustine, Florida

*Memories of Mayberry, A Nostalgic Look At Andy Griffith's Hometown: Mount Airy, North Carolina.* Copyright © 2001 by Jewell Mitchell Kutzer. All rights reserved. No part of this book may be used, reproduced or transmitted in any form or by any means, electronic or mechanical, including photocopying or recording, or by any information storage and retrieval system, without written permission, except in the case of brief quotations embodied in articles or reviews. For information, contact the publisher: Dynamic Living Press, P.O. Box 3164, St. Augustine, FL 32085-3164.

This hardcover edition of *Memories of Mayberry, A Nostalgic Look At Andy Griffith's Hometown: Mount Airy, North Carolina* features a "self-jacket" that eliminates the need for a separate dust jacket. It provides sturdy protection for your book while it saves paper, trees and energy.

Cover and interior design and formatting by Mayapriya Long, Bookwrights.com
Cover art and illustrations © Edwin A. Camin, unless otherwise noted.
Used with permission.
Photos by the author, unless otherwise noted.

Library of Congress Cataloging-in-Publication Data


Kutzer, Jewell Mitchell.
    Memories of Mayberry, A Nostalgic Look At Andy Griffith's Home-
town: Mount Airy, North Carolina / Jewell Mitchell Kutzer
        p.      cm.
    Includes Index
    Library of Congress Control Number: 2001117648
    ISBN 0-9711000-4-7
    1. The Andy Griffith Show (Television program)-
       Miscellanea
    2. Mount Airy (N.C.)
    3. Title.

    791.45'72 dc-20

# A Personal Word From the Author

THE WRITING OF THIS BOOK WAS a labor of love, for I have long wanted to write about the real town of Mount Airy, North Carolina, which was every bit as wonderful and as quirky as the fictional *Mayberry*. I also wanted to pay tribute to my grandfather, Judge A. E. Creed, who more than anyone else in my life, was responsible for giving me the ethics and values I try to live by.

Writing a non-fiction book based on a combination of research and memories brings both pleasures and pitfalls. As a writer, one of my favorite anecdotes has to do with two sisters, both of whom are well-known authors. (They shall remain anonymous to protect the guilty.)

It seems one of the sisters had written a chapter for her new book in which she described an event in her childhood, which also involved her mother and sister. When the author showed the draft to her sister, she was adamant in her criticism of the way the event had been portrayed; it didn't match the sister's memories at all.

In an effort to resolve which sister was "right," the two women took the manuscript to their mother. She listened to both of the sisters recite their different versions of what had happened, and said, "Goodness gracious, that isn't the way it happened at all," and proceeded to give a version of the event that was quite different from either of the sister's memories. The first sister decided to publish her book, with no editing of the chapter, saying she wasn't about to change what were *her* memories.

I spent many hours reviewing microfiche of *The Mount Airy News* archives; many more hours interviewing friends, relatives, and townspeople who lived through the era, in order to flesh out my remembrances of the time. I became keenly aware of my age, when I was told again and again names of people who could have helped me in my research, but unfortunately were no longer alive.

Evoking the feeling of life in Mount Airy during the days Andy and I were growing up is the heart of this book. For my friends, those I went to school and church with, I did my best to elicit the flavor of those times. My memories may not be accurate in every detail—but they surely are true.

## *Jewell Mitchell Kutzer*

This book is not connected with *The Andy Griffith Show,* nor has it been created, licensed, authorized, or endorsed by Mayberry Enterprises, Danny Thomas Enterprises, Andy Griffith, Viacom, Inc. or CBS, Inc. and their successors in interest.

# *Acknowledgments*

❖ To ANDY GRIFFITH, who not only never forgot the specialness of his hometown, but translated it in such a way that people all over the United States and, indeed, the world, were able to share in the experience.

❖ To the wonderful "All American" town of Mount Airy, North Carolina, where both Andy Griffith and I were fortunate to have been born and raised. Special thanks are given to the following, who provided significant time and effort and assisting the author in both remembrance and research:

Virginia Poore Leach, Jack Leach, Ruth Minnick, Emmett Forrest, Charles (Snappy Lunch) Dowell, Russell (Floyd's City Barber Shop) Hiatt, Tanya Rees, Ann Vaughn, Ralph Epperson, John Browne, Lucy Poore Browne, Estelle Greenwood Belton, Eleanor Collins Webster, Bill Holcomb, Tim Chadwick, Lucy Ellen Gwyn, Julie Smith, David Bradley and Pat Gwyn.

Also, the staff members of the following institutions were of considerable assistance to the author:

Mount Airy Public Library, Mount Airy Visitors' Center, Surry Arts Council and the Greater Mount Airy Chamber of Commerce.

A special note of appreciation to all those citizens of Mount Airy who were kind enough to let me stop them on Main Street and ask questions about both "the good old days" and the wonderful present in this special town.

❖ To Jim Clark, Head Goober of *The Andy Griffith Show* Rerun Watchers Club, who has used his love for the show to keep all of us informed and connected to the series and its characters.

To Allan (Floyd) Newsome, and the creator of the "Whose Messing Up the Bulletin Board" Internet Chapter. That site helps those all over the world to keep in touch in areas where there may be no organized chapters.

To all the delightful fans of The Andy Griffith Show who gave me helpful feedback on the contents of the book and loving support for the project.

❖ To my fellow professional members of the National Speakers Association who have given me ideas, information and support on this book, especially: Dottie Walters, Dan Poynter and Jeanne Robertson,Clare Rice and all the members of the North Florida Professional Speakers Association.

❖ To my family, friends and professional associates in St. Augustine, Florida, the oldest city in the United States, where I now reside.

To my family:

Ellen Davis, my daughter, who served as Editor, Prodder, and all-around Supporter. Couldn't have done it without her!

Pete Davis, my son-in-law, a long- time fan of *The Andy Griffith Show,* who was willing to share his tape collection with me. No wonder my daughter fell in love with him!

David Bradfield, my son, who never wavered in his belief in my abilities and the book, and supported both in every way.

Bill Bradfield, my son, who gave me positive feedback on the chapters as they developed.

Mel Kutzer, my husband, who understood my passion for the project and encouraged me to "go for it."

Seaside Scribblers Writers Group: Carolee Bertish, Irene Lombardo, Marcia Lang, Michael Wright, and Peter Mojo, who gave me invaluable input as the chapters developed.

Francis Keiser, Jim Melfi, Sandy Cooper, Tricia Price, Sue Middleton, Janis Williams, Beth Pearce, Sheryl Aycock, Alison Ratovick, and Carl S. Horner, Associate Professor of American Literature, Flagler College, St. Augustine, Florida, and the members of his Portfolio and Creative Writing Workshop.

The reference staff of the St. Johns County Main Library, especially Cheryl Hirschi, whose knowledge was invaluable in coordinating technical aspects of the book.

❖ All the people I met who said, "I loved *The Andy Griffith Show,* but I never knew there was real town that had any connection to *Mayberry.*" **Now You Know!**

**Jewell Mitchell Kutzer** is a native of Mount Airy, North Carolina and grew up there during the same era as Andy Griffith.

Jewell is a freelance writer and professional speaker. She is an active member of the *National Speakers Association* and *Meeting Professionals International*.

For information about presentations on this book and relevant topics, go to: www.memoriesofmayberry.com

# Contributor Information

The author is especially indebted to the following persons, whose generosity in sharing of their talents and resources contributed greatly to this book.

For permission to include his paintings and drawings:
**Edwin A. Camin**

Mr. Camin is a self-taught artist specializing in oil/oil pastel portraits and watercolor pen and ink drawings. For information about his work and its availability contact:

Edwin A. Camin
1904 Main Street
Mount Airy, NC 270030-2404
Website: www.ed-camin.com
E-Mail: camin@ed-camin.com

For permission to reproduce and draw from articles in *The Mount Airy News,* published since 1880:
**George W. Summerlin**, Publisher
*The Mount Airy News*
319 Renfro
Mount Airy, NC 27030

For permission to quote a portion of his poem, *Mayberry*:
**George H. Randall**

Mr. Randall has written a number of poems relating to the area. For information on them and their availability contact:

George H. Randall
207 Inglewood Rd.
Mount Airy, NC 27030
Phone: (336) 320-2404

# *The Andy Griffith Show*

## Also Known As

# TAGS

THROUGHOUT THE YEARS, many of the fans of *The Andy Griffith Show* have come to refer to the show by its acronym: TAGS. At the end of a number of the chapters in this book, there is a section entitled, "TAGS Notes."

In that section information will be given on the numbers and titles of various episodes of *The Andy Griffith Show* in which people or events were mentioned that coordinate in some way with the information given in the chapter. The episode numbers are in the order they were filmed.

It is not suggested that the real events directly influenced the writing of the episodes. The author describes people and events that were part of life in Mount Airy while Andy Griffith was growing up there. It has been acknowledged by Andy, and the writers and directors of the show, that he drew on his background and experiences to give the show its "down-home" flavor.

Other writers have mentioned that real names and places from the Mount Airy area appear in the show. The author, who grew up in Mount Airy during the same years, has discovered additional connections. Many of these are revealed in the regular chapters, with others indicated in Section Seven.

NOTE: This is surely not a complete compilation. Fans that are aware of other TAGS episodes that have similarities to real events are encouraged to contact the publisher for potential inclusion in future editions of the book.

# Contents

# *Preface*

THE SNAPPY LUNCH, THE GRAND THEATER, the City Barber Shop: all were a familiar part of my childhood in Mount Airy, North Carolina. They were also a part of Andy Griffith's childhood, and he brought them to life in a town named *Mayberry* in the television classic, *The Andy Griffith Show*, and its sequel, *Mayberry R.F.D.*

In an interview some years ago, Andy Griffith remarked that no real town could actually be *Mayberry*, since everybody's problems were solved in thirty minutes. That's true, but as it says on a local post card; "If There's A *Mayberry*, Mount Airy Was Its Mentor." In addition to including actual locations and names of real people, much of the atmosphere of Mount Airy, and the congeniality of its residents shone through in every episode of the television series.

Although the show was set in the '50s and '60s, Andy Griffith, as well as the show's producers, acknowledged that special features were included in the series to evoke the feeling of earlier decades. For instance, I was struck by the use of a candlestick phone, and Sarah, the operator who knew everything about everybody. That was exactly the kind of phone I grew up with, and our operator, Millie, was just as knowledgeable.

I would barely have my request for a number out of my mouth when Millie would say, "Honey, there's no use for me to ring Mary Nell's house; Mizz Parker just told Mizz Harkrader that her whole family was goin' out for a ride and wouldn't be back for 'bout an hour or so."

Unfortunately, the personal touch had been replaced by a dial phone, with no local operator, long before the years represented on *The Andy Griffith Show*.

Viewers will also notice that many of the prices quoted in the show are reminiscent of the costs in the '30s and '40s. In various episodes we were told that a bar of candy cost 5 cents; a sundae only 10 cents at the drugstore; a room at the *Mayberry Hotel* with a bath costs $2.50 — all prices much lower than those charged in the late '50s and early '60s. Perhaps Andy was longing for those good old days in the early '40s, when he could buy a bologna sandwich at "The Snappy Lunch" for only 5 cents.

In the early episodes of *The Andy Griffith Show*, Sheriff Andy Taylor was also called upon to act as Justice of the Peace. When Andy was growing up in Mount Airy, my grandfather, Anderson Edward Creed, was serving as the *real* Justice of the Peace and United States Marshal in the town. Grandfather's office was upstairs over the police station and jail, and from time to time he would leave me with the officers on duty while he took care of some official matters. I loved playing checkers with the policemen, and they spoiled me with candy and over-filled cones of my favorite lemon custard ice cream. I was given free run of the place, except for the jail area in the back. Of course, it was the forbidden jail that fascinated me most.

One day, when the officers were busy, I sneaked into the shadowy jail area. The cells were empty. I went into the nearest one and lay down on the cot. It was dark, damp, and delightfully spooky being behind bars. I made believe that I had been arrested; it was an exciting idea to a seven-year old. Besides, surely a handsome prince would come and rescue me. No prince showed up, though — and it wasn't long before I began to scare myself!

Fortunately, I was able to sneak back into the police station before anyone realized I had been gone. Fans can visit that same jail today in Mount Airy, complete with a cell ready for *Otis*, and a picnic basket from *Aunt Bee*.

I invite you to come with me on a nostalgic journey.

Go back in time to the '30s and '40s in the small town of Mount Airy, nestled in the foothills of the Blue Ridge mountains. Experience the people and the events that were taking place there as Andy Griffith was growing up. Discover real folks as lovable and as quirky as the fictional ones. Return to more innocent days, when a person's word could be counted on, and people just naturally looked after one another.

Along the way you will find new insights into how Mount Airy and the surrounding area may have influenced both the creation of *Mayberry* and the character of *Sheriff Andy Taylor.*

Have A Right Nice Journey!

## Jewell Mitchell Kutzer

## TAGS *Notes:*

Episode

#108  "Opie & His Merry Men"
# 170  "A Man's Best Friend"
# 218  "Opie's Most Unforgettable Character"
Andy, Opie, Barney, Goober, and Floyd are shown playing checkers at the station at various times in the above episodes

# 155  "The Arrest of the Fun Girls"
Daphne and Skippy like to "play jail"
R. F. D. stood for Rural Free Delivery, a service President F. D. Roosevelt put in place to provide free mail service to addresses located in the country.

# SECTION ONE

# Welcome To Mayberry, The Friendly Town

"When you walk the streets that Andy walked
The many sights that you will see
Will leave no doubt as to what inspired him
To make his hometown Mayberry . . ."

Excerpted from *"Mayberry"*
By George H. Reynolds
© 1992 Used with permission

"Griffith used his North Carolina hometown as a model for Mayberry, basing many of the show's characters on the friends, neighbors and shopkeepers he grew up with...The idealized values espoused on '50s sitcoms are very much in evidence here."
—*Washington Post*

"Mount Airy may not exactly be Mayberry, but it definitely offers that little piece of home that all of us long for. It truly brings to mind the description Andy Griffith himself gave it: 'A kind of Camelot.' "
—*Family Motor Coaching*

Pilot Mountain—the town is its namesake. Known as "Mount Pilot" on *The Andy Griffith Show,* it is located just 14 miles south of Mount Airy on Highway 52.

# 1 From *Andy Griffith* to *Andy Taylor:* From *Mount Airy* to *Mayberry*

"WELL, WHAT DO YOU KNOW!" I called out to my family. "Andy Griffith is gonna have his own TV show." It was 1960 and it had just been announced that a new comedy series on CBS would bear Andy Griffith's name. I had a special interest in the show: Andy and I shared the same hometown, Mount Airy, North Carolina. We had grown up during the same era, gone to the same schools, and had some of the same mentors. Now he was going to star in a major TV series. It was a real story of "hometown boy makes good!"

Throughout the years, I had closely followed Andy's entertainment career. Although he was several years older than I was, our mutual love of music and theater brought me into contact with him from time to time during my school years. The minister of the Moravian church, Dr. E.T. Mickey, was also the choir director at Central Methodist Church where my family attended. The Moravian service took place early on Sunday morning, and as soon as it was completed, Dr. Mickey would hurry down to Central Methodist, bringing Andy along to enrich the male section of our choir. To all of us young girls, most of the men singing in the choir were really *old*, and so the sight of a cute teenage boy brought us to church in record numbers.

Andy and I both attended Rockford Street Grammar School, and had some of the same teachers. I remember the valiant efforts of Miss Coleman, our music teacher, to get the large group of nervous young people arranged properly on the auditorium stage for the year-end festival. Once we were assembled, she enthusiastically led us in her favorite choral piece, beaming as we raised our voices in song: "Welcome, sweet springtime . . ."

In interviews throughout the years, Andy Griffith has acknowledged that those grammar school programs provided him his first experiences performing on stage.

In 1946, Dr. Clifford Bair, the President of the National Opera Society, was brought in from Winston-Salem to lift the standards of the music department at the high school. Even though Andy was already a college student in Raleigh, Dr. Bair had heard of his talent. He continued the encouragement Dr. Mickey had given Andy, bringing him home from time to time to play special parts in the newly formed Mount Airy Opera Club. As an avid music student myself, I went with my friends backstage at the Rockford Street School Auditorium during rehearsals of "The Bartered Bride," a presentation that showcased Andy's music and comedy talent. We were a gaggle of giggling girls trying to get the attention of the cute "college man," hanging around each day until the stage manager shooed us off.

Word would drift back to Mount Airy that Andy was involved in a great many plays in college and that he had decided to pursue music and theater as a career. The newspaper ran an item reporting that Andy had been selected to play Sir Walter Raleigh in "The Lost Colony," the official play of North Carolina.

In 1950 my family moved away from Mount Airy, but I still kept my eyes and ears open for news of Andy Griffith. Along with thousands of others, I laughed at "What It Was Was Football," and all of Andy's hilarious revisions of Shakespeare's works. I was proud and happy when he was such a success on Broadway in "No Time for Sergeants." A relative sent me the issue of *The Mount Airy News* with the picture of Andy riding in the parade celebrating his birthday. Also part of the festivities was a special screening of "A Face in the Crowd," at the old Earle Theater, now renamed the "Cinema."

Bringing a new view to everyday situations, Andy carried his own special blend of humor and humanity into all of his professional endeavors. Now he was going to have his own television show. Would it reflect anything of the small southern town we both knew so well?

⌘ ⌘

*The Andy Griffith Show*, set in the fictional town of *Mayberry*, debuted on television in 1960. By that time, a number of directors, producers and writers not originally from the South, were helping develop the show. Fortunately, their experience with other small towns, their sensitivity to the "feel" that the show was aiming for, and Andy's strong input and oversight of both the process and the product, gave the world a wonderful, warm-hearted series. The much-admired radio personality, Paul Harvey, once called *Mayberry* "a backwoods Brigadoon."

I watched *The Andy Griffith Show* every week, alert for any reference that would specifically remind me of our common North Carolina roots. In most episodes there were street names that I was accustomed to, as well as family names I recognized. Virtually all of the songs sung by Andy and *The Darlings* were ones that were very familiar to me. Many of the songs Andy played and sang on the show were in *The Golden Book of Songs*, which we used in every assembly at the Rockford Street School. I wonder if Andy kept a copy of that song book. I know I still have mine.

In one episode Roy's Laundry was mentioned, and immediately I pictured the laundry's location on Spring Street. That memory took me back into my little-girl body, weighted down with a cloth satchel full of books, walking up the Spring Street hill on my way to the Rockford Street School. No matter how cold the morning, I always felt warmer when I passed Roy Hutchen's Laundry. Blasts of steam, coming rhythmically out of the pipe on top of the tin roof, punctuated the frosty air, accompanied by the sound of laundry workers talking and laughing inside. Only a few more yards, and I'd reach the top of the hill, out of breath, and cross Rockford Street to join my friends on the playground until the opening bell rang.

Spring Street had such a steep hill that when snow fell, the police roped it off and prohibited all vehicle traffic, turning it into an exciting downhill slope for all the children in the neighborhood. Anyone who had a Flexible Flyer, or a big piece of tin, or even cardboard, would head to the top of the hill. The boys always pushed off quickly for an exhilarating ride over snow and ice, whooping with delight all the way to the bottom. Most of us girls took our own sweet time before making the frightening trip, sometimes inviting boys to share our sleds to keep us "safe" during the ride.

Even in the summer, when the street was open to traffic, some of the more aggressive boys would use it as a track to check out the speed of their homemade "soapbox derby" cars. It was always exciting to watch them—if only to see if they would make it through the Church Street intersection or end up crashed into the stop sign at the bottom of the Spring Street hill.

It was a good time to be a child, and Mount Airy was a good place in which to grow up. It was a period when children walked freely all over town; when neighbors and townspeople were comfortable pointing out to a child any inappropriate words or actions they might notice; and a time when the child would not only pay attention to the correction, but also thank the adult for it.

The geographic setting of *The Andy Griffith Show* was originally non-specific, but Andy felt that it needed touches of realism to make it believable. Drawing on his own youth in North Carolina, Mount Airy could easily become Mayberry; Pilot Mountain turned around to be Mount Pilot; while several other Carolina towns retained their original names.

But perhaps Andy Griffith's choices of names and places weren't made casually. All through the years, Andy had been close to his mother and father, Geneva and Carl Griffith. He always credited his mother with instilling in him a love of music, and his father with passing on to him the delight of storytelling. Andy's beloved mother, Geneva Nunn, had been born in a rural area of Virginia called "Mayberry," located just across the state line, only a few miles north of Mount Airy. Andy's grandmother, on his father's side, was born Sarah Frances Taylor. And so, Sheriff Andy Taylor, living in Mayberry, talking on the telephone to a woman named Sarah, was certain to keep the *fictional* Andy always feeling close to those the *real* Andy cared about.

Whatever the exact details of the show's development, it is certain that the imaginary town seemed like a real one, and its inhabitants displayed the variety of personalities found in many small towns. The show's sense of place, the use of real-life models for some characters and businesses, and the atmosphere of strong values and ethics are some of the reasons that the town of *Mayberry* itself became a major character in the series.

Of course, Mount Airy *was* different from *Mayberry*. Andy must have had those differences in mind when they were filming the two episodes, "Taylors in Hollywood" and "The Hollywood Party" during the sixth season. Fans will remember that the whole family had gone out to California to film, "Sheriff Without a Gun," based on Sheriff Andy Taylor's life in *Mayberry*.

Aunt Bee was appalled when she found out that the movie wouldn't depict Andy handing out Christmas presents or giving safety talks, but rather planned to show Andy in a barroom brawl. She was also upset that they called *Mayberry* "Blueberry," and that the location of the town was given as being in South Carolina. Her attitude softened, however, when she found out that the movie would portray her as young and alluring. After giving it much thought, Aunt Bee agreed that it was all right to change things around somewhat, in order to make the story *more interesting*.

When Sheriff Andy Taylor and his young son, Opie, go fishing; when Aunt Bee makes chicken and dumplings; when Barney and Floyd try to outdo each other, the spirit of Mount Airy is alive and well in *Mayberry*.

As Jim Clark, one of the founders of *The Andy Griffith Show* Rerun Watchers Club said, "Mount Airy's not exactly *Mayberry*, but it's about as close as you can get."

# TAGS *Notes:*

Episode

#23 "Andy and Opie, Housekeepers"
Spring Street

#52 "Barney and the Choir"
featuring "Welcome Sweet Springtime"

#55 "Aunt Bee the Warden"
Roy's Laundry

#136 "Opie's Fortune"
Opie roams alone freely all over town in this and virtually all episodes

#138 "The Pageant"
The town of Mayberry is said to have been established in 1864. Mount Airy was founded in 1885, and the author's great-grandfather, Anderson Creed was one of the town's original councilmen.

#154 "Aunt Bee's Invisible Beau"
Andy Griffith paid homage to his Mount Airy roots when Sheriff Taylor is seen reading a copy of *The Mount Airy News*.

#167 "Taylors In Hollywood"

#168 "The Hollywood Party"

❖ The Rockford Street Grammar School Auditorium has been renovated and renamed "The Andy Griffith Playhouse." It serves as a cultural center for the area and during "Mayberry Days," it is the site of functions, food and fun! More information can be found in Section Six.

❖ *Mount Pilot* is referred to frequently throughout the series. The real town is named Pilot Mountain, and lies just 14 miles south of Mount Airy. The major change from reality is that Pilot Mountain has always been much smaller than Mount Airy. In TAGS, *Mount Pilot* is represented as a much larger and more sophisticated city, where the residents of *Mayberry* go to get things not available at home.

# 2 | *Searching for a Sheriff*

*"You gotta understand. This is a small town. The sheriff is more than just a sheriff. He's a friend."*

—Deputy Barney Fife

IN THE SPRING OF 1942, like many other Mount Airy young people, Andy Griffith could probably be found walking up Main Street with his friends. The sights and sounds announcing local elections couldn't be missed. There were signs on every corner and speeches in every hall.

I found elections exciting. My grandfather never tired of talking about politics, and I was being raised with both enthusiasm and respect for the process. I remember Grandfather saying, in an exaggeration of the local dialect, "Yes-suh—ya sho' can tell it's election time! When a feller sticks his hand out thuh winder of the car to signal a left turn, he'll most likely have three or four candidates come up and pump his hand 'fore he can git 'round the corner."

That spring, Sheriff H. S. Boyd thought he was set for another term until something a mite unusual happened. Three other candidates decided to challenge Boyd for the Democratic nomination. Two were well-known local politicos, but the third, Sam Patterson, was an unknown with no political background. In the beginning, nobody much was sure who Sam was, and then bits and pieces of information began to make the rounds at the Oddfellows' meetings and among the fellers lollygaggin' on the Post Office steps.

"Hey, ain't that thuh same guy that works as a night watchman down at the furniture factory?" One citizen after another asked the question until the answer came back.

"Derned if it ain't—but what's he doing runnin' for Sheriff?"

It was a good question, seeing as how it was said that Sam could neither read nor write. As the story came out, a bunch of folks were mighty unhappy with the way Sheriff Boyd had handled his position. They convinced Sam to run against the Sheriff and paid his filing fee.

It started out as a joke, just to give Sheriff Boyd something to think about. But they hadn't counted on how Sam would be affected. Just going along for the fun of it at the beginning, Sam took to the attention he was getting and started thinking and acting like a serious candidate.

Through the years Sam had learned a trick or two to disguise his lack of education. He had a sharp mind and could memorize just about anything. Once he had met a man, and been introduced to his family, whenever he came upon him later, he could call him by name and accurately call the names of his children, adding some complimentary remark about the man's work or reputation.

In no time at all, people were saying nice things about Sam Patterson and how he just might make a decent sheriff. They were especially pleased with the way he spent more time listening than talking, and more time asking than telling.

Sam was a God-fearing man. He made a point of attending the Wednesday night prayer meetings of all the churches in the county. Eyes lifted to the heavens, he belted out, "A-ma-z-ing Grace, how suh-weet thuh sound, that suh-aved a-ah wretch like me." Friends remarked that Sam's untrained voice was sounding better than ever. "It's almost as if some kind of a-nointin' is tak'n place."

Weddings, funerals, baptisms, Sunday School picnics—Sam believed that whenever two or three were gathered in Jesus' name, he ought to be there also. Although Sam had never learned to drive, his supporters gladly took him every place he wanted to go. In those days, country churches had all-day meetings on the grounds, featuring an array of home-cooked specialties provided by the ladies of the congregation. Sam never missed a one, piling his plate high with fried chicken, sweet 'taters, okra, and corn bread. He was said to eat a full meal with each group, so as to compliment the ladies on their cooking. On occasion, he would ask for food to take home to his family, a request which was happily filled.

Even his critics admitted Patterson struck an imposing figure. He was well over six feet tall, with strong features, a ruddy complexion, and the enormous size of his feet was the topic of much conversation.

When he took on the Sheriff's race, Sam was middle-aged with a large family, some of the boys already grown to manhood. Everybody in the family pitched in to support the effort to elect him, fanning out over the county so as not to miss any event where there might be voters.

Patterson did all his campaigning directly with the people, even though the other candidates sought to influence opinion with paid ads in *The Mount Airy News*. Interest in the Sheriff's race was high, which the newspaper acknowledged, opining, "It was admitted that each will pull a good vote as all have made a hard campaign in the county."

On the day of the May Democratic primary, Sheriff Boyd pulled 1,595 votes and Sam garnered 1,261 votes, putting the two men into a Democratic run-off election to be held in June. The newspaper reported that Sheriff Boyd said he had not campaigned actively in the primary, but planned a strong effort for the run-off election. The paper went on to state, "Patterson is letting no grass grow under his No.17 shoes, and was found attending birthday celebrations Sunday afternoon in a rural section of the county."

Sam's supporters eventually took out ads in the paper prior to the run-off, emphasizing that, "If elected Sheriff, Sam Patterson enters upon his duties without his hands tied by promises and commitments to any group or faction. He will enforce our laws without fear or favoritism."

Sam added his personal pledge, "I promise to execute the duties of Sheriff in such a manner that you will have no reason to regret the fact that you supported me."

In the weeks before the run-off, Patterson continued his steady involvement with the people and their interests. Arriving on the scene of a gathering, Sam would make a beeline for the young'uns, making sure no baby missed his kissing and cuddling before moving on to shake the hands of everyone present.

The churches in the mountain area were well known for a special ceremony they held. Parishioners reenacted the story of Jesus washing the feet of his disciples, signifying that He was a servant, not a master. Sam Patterson was an enthusiastic participant in every foot-washing ceremony in the surrounding communities. The sight of Sam, kneeling and humbly washing feet, conveyed the image of a man willing to serve the people in a way no campaign rhetoric could have accomplished.

It was a dumbfounded Sheriff Boyd who shook his head over the run-off election results. More people voted than in the primary and Sam Patterson received more than twice the number of votes cast for Boyd, easily claiming the Democratic nomination. Sam went on to win handily over the Republican candidate in the general election in November to win election as Sheriff.

Sam Patterson served as Sheriff of Surry County for twelve years, surviving election challenges many times. He continued his practice of mingling with the masses. With a deputy at the wheel, Sam regularly covered the county and was said to know the name of each and every citizen.

Sam's lack of education no longer seemed an obstacle, but remained a source of friendly ribbing. When asked, "Now how is it you spell your first name, Sam?" he would reply, "Just like it sounds, C A M," and good-natured laughter from all would follow.

During all his years of service, Sheriff Patterson had respect for the individual citizens of the communities he served, stayed close to the people, and treated everyone impartially.

❖❖

- ❖ The premise of the 1986 television movie, "Return to Mayberry" was that Sheriff Patterson had died and Andy Taylor was considering running again for sheriff.

- ❖ One of the hallmarks of Andy's portrayal of Mayberry's sheriff was the caring and supportive attitude of Sheriff Taylor toward all the people of the area. Perhaps it is more than a coincidence that Mount Airy's Sheriff Sam Patterson was a role model for that kind of behavior.

❖ Sheriff Sam Patterson's presence in Andy Griffith's formative years was also mentioned in one of Paul Harvey's radio broadcasts of "The Rest Of the Story."

Right:
Poore's Grocery Store

**YOUR FEET ARE**
*In Clover*
**WHEN THEY'RE IN**
**WOLVERINE**
*Shell* **HORSEHIDES**
*SEE THAT SHELL*

**WOLVERINE**
SHELL HORSEHIDE WORK SHOES

**$2.98 to $4.50**

*Boyles*
— SHOE STORE —
MOUNT AIRY, N. C.

You'll have no regrets with
**HANES** WINTER SETS
We have all sizes and styles
**BELK'S Dept. STORE**
N. Main St.          Mount Airy, N. C.

*Again*
**DR. MILES**
**NERVINE**
*—makes good*

Hundreds Of Thousands Of Times
Each Year Dr. Miles Nervine
Makes Good

When you are wakeful, jumpy,
restless, when you suffer from *Nervous Irritability, Nervous Headache,
Sleeplessness, or Excitability,* give
**DR. MILES NERVINE**
a chance to make good for YOU.

Don't wait until nerves have kept
you awake two or three nights,
until you are restless, jumpy and
cranky. Get a bottle of Dr. Miles
Nervine the next time you pass a
drug store. Keep it handy. You
never know when you or some
member of your family will need it.

*At Your Drug Store:*
Small Bottle    25¢
Large Bottle   $1.00

Dr. Miles Nervine is also made in Effervescent Tablet from.

NERVOUS AND BLUE
READS ABOUT DR. MILES NERVINE
BUYS AND TRIES IT
WRITES ENTHUSIASTIC LETTER

# 3 | *Main Street as Andy Knew It*

IT PROBABLY IS DIFFICULT for today's young people to understand the joy previous generations felt just walking up and down Main Street. Every small town had a "Main Street" which served as the center of activity in the town. In Mount Airy, Main Street was the center of the town and a kaleidoscope of delights for its people.

I am sure Andy Griffith has many recollections of the places he and his friends frequented. In those days children as young as 6 years old walked freely all over town as long as it was daytime. As I was growing up, I made many trips up and down Main Street, picking up items for the family, window shopping, or just "hanging out" with my friends. However, many of my favorite memories are of the wonderful walks with my grandfather, Judge A. E. Creed, up and down Main Street as it was in the early 1940s.

Let your mind's eye travel with me as we encounter some of Main Street's delights, as I remember seeing them with my grandfather, as well as on my wanderings alone.

## Poore's Grocery Store

On the south end of Main Street, where it crossed West Pine Street, was Poore's Store, owned by distant cousins. It was a true family business, having been started by Floyd Poore in 1891. Now the business was being run by his son, Walter, and his wife, Doris. I never ran out of things to see in that store. Every inch of space was taken up with appealing displays and aromatic delights.

One of the real treats for me was when Cousin Walter would let me go into the back room to watch the other employees "candle" eggs. They called it that because in the past, candles had been used in the process. Now each egg was held up to a bare light bulb, which let you look through the thin eggshell and check to see if the yolk was alright. He explained that they were making sure there were no clots of blood around the yolk, or a cloudy look to the egg white that would mean that the egg wasn't good. Once in awhile, he would let me hold an egg in front of the light bulb. "Well, what do ya think, Jewell—is that one fit to eat?" After a while I learned to pick out the bad ones easily, and it was a skill I was very proud of.

Grandfather loved dill pickles. As soon as we got in the grocery store, he would head for the pickle barrel and select a plump juicy one, munching on it as we picked out items to be added to our written order, which would later be delivered to the house. When Cousin Doris tallied up the total to be added to our family's charge account, Grandfather would always say, "Now, Doris, don't forgit to add on that de-licious pickle I just et."

Doris would smile and say, "I don't rightly think I see a pickle, Judge Creed, and I can't charge you for something I don't see."

"Much obliged." With a smile and a nod, Grandfather would lick his lips, pat his stomach, and the ritual would be complete.

During my years at Rockford Street Grammar School, I went almost every day to the grocery store to pick up bread or some other small item for my mother or grandparents. Each time I would get myself a nickel candy bar and have it added to the order.

After many months of this routine, one day when Doris was totaling up the items, she turned to me and very pleasantly asked, "Jewell, does your mother know you are buying a candy bar every day?"

I took a deep breath and tried to appear unconcerned. "I don't know if she does or not. I'm not sure I have mentioned it to her." I hoped my voice didn't betray the shaking I felt inside my body.

"Well, honey, she might not want you to have that much candy; it's not really good for your teeth, you know. You might want to check with her before you buy any more." Doris continued to smile as she packed the items in a small brown sack.

"Yes, Ma'am, I will." I grabbed the sack and got out of there as fast as I could. Doris and my mother were good friends and talked frequently. I really hoped she wouldn't say anything to Mother before I got a chance.

I mulled over the situation as I walked very slowly down South Main Street, past the high school, turning at the Presbyterian Church and down the Church Street hill to my grandparents' home. Mother would be there soon. I didn't want to tell her. I was afraid to tell her, but Cousin Doris wouldn't let me have any more candy until I gave her an okay from Mother. I tried to find a good time to talk with Mother that evening after we had gotten back to our apartment, but I never could get the words out of my mouth.

I avoided going back to Poore's for several days. When I finally did, I walked in, picked up a loaf of bread, took it to the clerk to be thin-sliced, and then, acting as casually as I could manage, brought the bread over to Cousin Doris at the counter.

"Well, hello, Jewell. I haven't seen you around the past few days. By the way, how's your Mother doing these days?" Doris tipped her head and displayed her ever-present smile.

I answered her using my strongest, brightest voice, accompanied by my best Shirley Temple grin. "Oh, she's fine, Mizz Poore. And by the way, I asked her about my charging a candy bar every day, and she agrees with you that it probably wouldn't be good for my teeth. She says 3 candy bars a week should be enough for me to have. I think I'll take an Almond Joy today, if you please."

Walking home, I tried to swallow the "story" with the candy. The chocolate and nuts were *delicious*! And so, I found out years later, was the laughter between my mother and Doris, who had Millie ring Mother on the phone as soon as I left the store.

Although by the mid-forties large grocery chains such as Kroger, A.& P. and Piggly-Wiggly had moved onto Main Street, with advertising specials, shopping carts, and "low prices," Poore's Grocery remained in business until 1950, when Walter Poore's health finally caused the closing of the store and the ending of an era.

## Snappy Lunch

Just a few doors up the street was a wonderful spot for good food and good conversation, the "Snappy Lunch." Since it has been in existence since 1929, is still in operation, and was specifically mentioned on *The Andy Griffith Show*, I have given it a chapter all its own in Section Six.

## Creed's Book Store

Although no longer active in the book and stationery business, Grandfather never failed to point out to me where the family business, Creed's Book Store, had been located, just a few doors north of the Snappy Lunch. His father's brother, J. W. Creed, had established it in the early 1900s, and it was in continuous operation until 1926. Various other family members had run the store over the years until my grandfather took over its operation after the death of his brother, Will Creed.

In those days all the high school students were required to buy their books, and Creed's had been designated as the official book store by the State of North Carolina. In addition to textbooks, there were glass enclosed counters displaying stationery, pens and other sundry items. There was a soda fountain that drew many young people year round. My mother had worked in the store, and reported that when the students came to get their books just before the start of the school year, "you couldn't stir 'em with a stick."

On a recent visit to Mount Airy I spoke with a lady in her 80s who clearly remembered Grandfather and Creed's Book Store.

"He was such skinny man—climbing up that rolling ladder to get us books from the shelf near the ceiling. I was really afraid he would fall, but thank goodness he didn't. Just brought down that pile of books from the top shelf steady as you please!"

## City Barber Shop

Many times as a young girl, I sat and waited for my grandfather to get his hair cut in that barber shop. It was the same kind of gathering place as was represented on *The Andy Griffith Show*. Since it was one of the focal points of the show, it is described in detail in Section Six.

## Wolfe's Drug Store

Farther up Main Street was Wolfe's Drug Store. In addition to prescription drugs, its shelves were crammed with popular remedies and beauty potions. I remember the floor space being crowded with wooden tables holding daily "specials."

Grandfather had me practice my reading and comprehension skills everywhere we went. Pointing to an item on the shelf, the exercise would begin, "Look here, honey, what does that box say?"

I remember one time it was a black and white box that was the focus of his attention. I took it down from the shelf in order to get a closer look at it.

" 'Miles Ner-vine,' Did I say it right, Grandfather?"

Grandfather smiled and patted me on the head. "That's close. It looks like it should be 'vine,' but it's pronounced Ner-veen. What else does it say on the box?"

"This bottle costs a whole dollar. Why does it cost so much?"

He laughed and replied, "Well, just look at the ingredients, honey. It's got a purty good dose of alcohol in it. And here we are in a dry county. Reckon it's a big seller for the store."

Not only reading, but also logic and moral commentary were part of every day's experience with my grandfather.

## Lamm's Drug Store

I always thought it funny that we had drugstores named Wolfe's and Lamm's. Just like their names, they were entirely different in their approach to business. While the emphasis at Wolfe's was on merchandising, Lamm's brought in customers by making it a fun place to be.

There was a wonderful soda fountain, dispensing an array of milkshakes, cherry Cokes, banana splits and chocolate nut sundaes. Oh, those sundaes, overflowing with rich vanilla ice cream, creamy delicious chocolate syrup, sticky-sweet pecans, and a passel of real whipped cream, topped off with a big maraschino cherry. And not a single, solitary soul mentioning anything about too many calories or gaining weight. Dear Lord, take me back to those days!

The drugstore had a half-dozen small round marble tables with wrought-iron legs, surrounded by four matching chairs sporting a swirled design which came to be known as "Coke" chairs. They were frequently filled with giggling girls and attentive boys, partaking of sweet delights while sharing secrets and schemes.

I loved having lunch with Grandfather at Lamm's Drug Store. The people behind the counter were cheerful and easygoing. They didn't even have to ask me what I wanted when we came in, but nodded and smiled in our direction and began immediately to fix my favorite, a grilled cheese sandwich. Grandfather preferred ham and cheese with a Dr. Pepper. My favorite was Coca-Cola, freshly prepared by mixing dark, sweet syrup and sparkling carbonated water from the soda fountain.

No doubt about it, Lamm's Drugstore was the place to hang out. The wide aisles, bright colors, and smiling clerks all seemed to be saying, "Ya' all come on in and set a spell."

## Boyles Shoe Store

On the east side of Main was Boyles Shoe Store, selling shoes for all the family. The owners and store clerks emphasized what we now call "customer service," but then it meant helping the customer find what was desired and treating him or her pleasantly and courteously, just because it was the right thing to do. The clerks really helped you get shoes that *fit* and were *comfortable*. Check out this news brief that appeared on the front page of *The Mount Airy News*:

"Boyd Gardner of Asheville has arrived in the
city and is now a salesman for Boyles Shoe Store.
He is an experienced shoe fitter."

I remember Mother and I shopping at Boyles. The men that waited on us took all the time that was necessary to check and recheck the position of the foot to make sure the shoe would be comfortable to wear.

No wonder our feet hurt today! When is the last time you can remember working with a shoe salesperson who had actually been *trained* to fit shoes properly?

Boyles also had the latest in technology for those times. There was a machine that you stood on that looked like a "your weight for a penny" machine, and carried the "Red Goose" shoe logo. Instead of looking in the top and seeing how much you weighed— you saw an x-ray picture of your feet in the shoes you were considering buying.

The intent of the foot x-ray machine was to help determine if there was sufficient room in the shoe for your toes to move around. It was fascinating to wiggle my toes and see them move in the image. Just imagine! I could see the skeleton of my own feet!

You don't see those kinds of machines in shoe stores any more. I guess the main reason is that as we learned more about the effect of x-rays, we became more cautious as to how continued exposure might affect the clerks in the store and the customers who might use the machine frequently. Frankly, most of us children, myself included, popped into the shoe store several times a week just to see what our feet looked like. It sure was fun while it lasted!

## Eating Places

There were other eating facilities in the Main Street area during those years, some in business for many years, others just a few: Jimmie's Cafe, The Canteen, Johnson's Cafe, Belton Cafe, Main Street Grill, Laurence Lunch, Times Square Lunch, Gibson Ice Cream Parlor, and probably others I have forgotten. One of the businesses that was on Main Street was the Blue Bird Cafe. It must have stood out in Andy's memory, and so the Blue Bird Diner came to life in *Mayberry*.

## Auto Supply Stores

Goober would have had many places to buy any auto parts he needed in Mount Airy during the '30s and '40s. On Main Street alone there were four auto supply stores: Economy Auto Supply, Firestone Auto Store, Western Auto Store, and Hylton's Auto

Supply. In addition, there were three tire stores: Town Tire Service, Master Tire Service, and Clark Tire Shop.

## Movie Theaters

There were three wonderful theaters. The Grand was the largest and was located on the west side of Main Street and the Earle and Center were on the east side. Read all about them in Section One, Chapter 4.

## Clothing Stores/Department Stores

In the late '30s and early '40s a number of small clothing stores did business on Main Street. Locals may remember: The Charles Store, Efrids, S & W Clothing, Blue Ridge Clothing, Dixie Clothing, Harrison's Department Store, and Leon's, which had ladies' and children's clothes.

One of the special things about these stores was that my mother and I could go in, look over the merchandise, pick out two or three outfits apiece and take them home "on approval." We would then try them on in the privacy of our home, and check them out with various shoe and jewelry combinations. I would parade my dresses in front of Grandmother to get her opinion on which ones to keep. We'd keep any that suited us, and return the rest to the store within a few days. It was a wonderful system.

During the mid-forties, department store chains began to open up in Mount Airy, putting both a J. C. Penney and Belk's on Main Street. While shopping at those stores lacked much of the personal service of the smaller stores, the lower prices offered as a result of volume buying did draw local customers into the stores.

I was fascinated by the way you paid for items purchased at Penney's. After you took your choices of merchandise to the clerk at a central counter, she would write a description of the items and their prices down on a piece of paper. Then the order slip and the cash offered, were put it into a container that fit into a clear glass tube leading to an office upstairs. A "whooshing" sound would accompany the tube as it was drawn upward and out of sight. After a few minutes it would miraculously return to the bottom of the glass tube at the counter with a loud thud. The clerk would take the order slip out and give the change back to my mother, along with the merchandise that had been wrapped and tied with a colorful bow while we were waiting. I found the process so intriguing that when I was uptown for other things, I would stop in Penney's just to watch the "glass tube show." (No credit cards existed in those days and checks were mainly used when paying bills that needed to be mailed.)

When Belk's opened up in town, they brought with them an innovation that drew many people to the store. The sign on Belk's window read "Air Cooled," and everybody wanted to see just what that meant. As I opened their front door, I felt a blast of cool air rise from my feet past my head. A young, blond woman clerk responded to my obvious surprise with a smile and an explanation.

"Doesn't that feel good, honey? There's air blowing across ice in the back room, and we've piped it up here so it cools you off the minute you come into the store. Be sure you tell the rest of your family how good that feels. We've got places all over the store that are pushing out cooled air so our customers can be more comfortable while they shop." She sounded as if she had repeated those words many times that day.

I wandered around for a while, checking out items I might tell my mother about. As I approached the front door to leave, the young clerk spoke to me again. "You won't forgit to tell your mother about this new store, will ya hon?"

"No ma'am, I'll tell her tonight," I promised. And I did, along with a recitation of the items I wanted her to buy.

## Hardware Stores

During Andy's youth there were four hardware stores on Main Street: Hayes Cash Hardware, Merritt Hardware, Midkiff Hardware, and Holcomb Hardware.

My grandfather always made it a point to stop in and "chew thuh fat" with the guys in the hardware stores. "I get the real lowdown from those men. They tell me what the people are really concerned about. It helps me both politicking and judging."

As Bill Holcolmb tells it, when you entered a hardware store in those days, the unmistakable smell of leather goods pervaded the air, reflecting the tanning operations on site. Stores that sold hardware were not only a necessity in those days, they served as gathering places for the men in the community—a place where tales could be told and friendships made, all while buyin' two screws and a nail.

Holcomb's Hardware is still in existence on Main Street, with wooden floors well-worn by sixty-five years of boots and country clay and silt. At Holcomb's you can still find wooden bins holding hundreds of metal items, barrels of nails, shelves with dozens of kinds of hammers, and clerks that still ask you what you want, and then go get it for you.

## The First National Bank

Most banks advertise that they are "strong as a rock." In the case of First National Bank, with a building made of granite, it was literally the case. Founded in 1898, the bank was a major financial presence in the community. As a child, I was fascinated by the 8 ft. high round brass door, covering a walk-in safe. It, and the clock outside, were well-recognized symbols of Mount Airy.

Today that building is occupied by the Chamber of Commerce, and the imposing safe is walk-in file storage. The clock is still in operation and a representation of the antique timepiece is a part of the official "Welcome To Mount Airy" logo.

## TAGS Notes:

Episode

#85    "The Great Filling Station Robbery"
       Juanita works at the Blue Bird Diner

#154   "Aunt Bee's Invisible Beau"
       Evan Hendricks, the butter and egg man's son, is seen "candling" eggs.

#160   "Opie's Job"
       People "called in" orders, the grocery owner, Mr. Doakes, filled the orders, and Opie and Billy delivered the orders to the homes. Goober takes an apple from an outside display, bites into it and calls in to Mr. Doakes to, "put it on my bill."

# 4 | Let's Go to the Picture Show

WHEN ANDY AND I WERE GROWING UP in Mount Airy, the only way you could see a film was to go to the "movin' pitcher show." Going to the movies was the major source of entertainment out of the home.

As I think about it now, it is amazing that in 1940 there were three active movie theaters in Mount Airy, a town of only 4,000 residents. The Grand and the Earle were the largest, but the Center Theater was the place where all the kids hung out on Saturdays. There were matinees at 2 and 4, and most kids stayed through both of them. In addition to the feature film, there were cartoons, a Pathe newsreel, and sometimes a sing-along reel.

After wolfing down a hot dog and an Orange Crush at the Snappy Lunch, I'd go across the street, meet my friends, pay the 25¢ admission, grab a box of freshly buttered popcorn, and a couple of Mounds bars, and settle in for the afternoon. Children under 6 could get in for 10¢ apiece, but they had to be accompanied by a parent or other relative. The adults accompanying young children always entered the theater reluctantly, and left 4 hours later much the worse for wear. But for those of us in the 6 to 12 year old group, it was a giant party every Saturday.

There were the wonderful serials, where there was always a crisis at the end of the reel, and so we would *have* to come back next Saturday to see what happened. There were the high action cowboy sagas: Tom Mix, Hopalong Cassidy, Roy Rogers, and The Lone Ranger! We sang along with the Sons of the Pioneers and yelled "Hi Ho, Silver!" Cheers, groans, and screams rose up from the crowd in response to the action on the screen. If the audience thought a character was in danger, screams of warning would resound throughout the theater. The noise level was substantial and would continue to resonate in our ears long after we had left the theater. Only the bravest of the ushers were assigned to the Saturday matinees. For you younger folks reading this, think of it as a more innocent Rocky Horror Show crowd.

The Earle Theater was a little farther up the block on Main Street. It was elegantly decorated inside and could seat over 400 people. My mother loved going to picture shows and took me with her on many occasions. When I was five, the theater announced that Disney's *Snow White* would be shown there, and Mother had promised me that she would take me to see it. Unfortunately, when it finally opened in Mount Airy, I was not quite over a "flu bug" and was still weak. Grandmother cautioned Mother against taking me to the theater in my condition. Surprisingly, Mother didn't take her advice. She wrapped me in a sheet blanket and carried me into the theater.

"It'll make you feel better, Jewell." My mother believed that "getting away" from life's problems by going to the movies was good medicine.

I have another strong memory connected with the Earle Theater. When I was at Mount Airy High School, if it had been raining overnight and was still pouring in the morning, the classes would be shortened and school would be let out at 1 PM. The purpose was to insure that the busses carrying the students from the country areas would be able to get them home safely without getting stuck in the mud. This was a real plus for us who lived in town, as it gave us the opportunity to go to the matinee at the Earle.

On one rain-shortened school day all the older students had been buzzing about the movie that was showing at the Earle. It was

*The Outlaw*, starring Jane Russell and Jack Buetel. I had no idea what the film was about, but took the occasion to hang out with the older crowd and tag-a-long to the movie with them.

The flyers out front showed Jane Russell in a low-cut blouse with a sultry look on her face. (I didn't know what "sultry" meant then; I found out later. For those of you who don't remember what Jane Russell looked like, she went on to be the spokeswoman for the "18 Hour Bra for Full-Figured Women.")

The movie was in the new "Technicolor" with expansive western scenes, and told a story of a cowboy who was fleeing from the law. In one scene, Jack Buetel's character was very ill, cold and shaking all over. Jane Russell's character leaned over the bed and said in a low-pitched, breathy voice, "Don't worry - I'll keep you warm." She crawled into bed with him, pulled the covers over both of them and snuggled close to the shaking cowboy. There were gasps and giggles from the other students and the rest of the audience.

I wondered what the big deal was; she was just keeping him warm! Besides, in the next scene he looked as if he had fully recovered, and had a big smile on his face. As we were leaving the theater, I heard some of the others kids say that *The Outlaw* had been banned in a couple of countries, and they wondered how in the world it ever got shown in Mount Airy. I decided it might be best if I didn't mention to Mother where I spent my afternoon.

The Earle Theater still exists on Main Street in Mount Airy, but it has been renamed the "Cinema." When Andy Griffith's movie, *A Face in the Crowd*, was released, there was a special screening in that theater, as well as a big celebration, complete with bands, a parade, and the presentation of the "Key to the City" to Andy Griffith, scheduled to coincide with Andy Griffith's birthday.

Today, in addition to showing movies, the Cinema is the site for community gatherings. Each Saturday the theater hosts "The Merry-Go-Round," the longest-running radio show featuring bluegrass music. Sponsored by local radio station, WPAQ, it draws top-notch talent from a large area for the live performance. The show is free and the music is piped out onto Main Street for all to enjoy.

When Andy and I were growing up, the Grand Theater was quite a showplace. It was located on the south side of Main Street, across from the Earle. Both theaters had common ownership, and the management believed in advertising their superior facilities. In a newspaper advertising supplement with wide distribution, pictures of both theaters were shown, accompanied by the following text:

"In the Grand and Earle Theaters, operated and owned by Boone & Benbow, Mount Airy talking picture houses are second to no other city of much larger size in the country. Audiences for both theaters are drawn from two states. The Capacious Grand Theater has 739 seats, and is one of the few houses in the State equipped with 'Wide Range,' the latest improvement in the Production of Talking Pictures."

A local resident, Jack Leach, who worked for the theaters in their heyday, contributed some special insights into the early movie theater operations.

"I remember when the Earle got the right to show *Gone with the Wind.* The whole town was excited, and there was no way we could have gotten all the patrons into one theater. In those days, movie film was wrapped onto several reels, depending on the length of the show. So for the highly anticipated *GWTW*, they started the first reel at the Earle, and as soon as it was finished, the projectionist at the Earle would remove it, give it to me, and I would literally run the large bulky metal reel across the street and down the alley, up the outside stairs and into the projection booth at the Grand, so the movie could begin for patrons at the Grand. I ran back and forth all evening bringing the other reels over as quickly as I could so that the transfer time would be as short as possible."

Jack was somewhat younger and stronger in those days, but with the length of film required for *Gone With the Wind*, he *reel-ly* earned his money.

The old Grand Theater no longer exists in Mount Airy, but fortunately lives on in *The Andy Griffith Show*, as the frequently-mentioned *Mayberry Grand Theater.*

# TAGS *Notes*

Episode

#9     "Andy the Matchmaker"
       Snappy Lunch

#50    "Jailbreak"
#78    "The Bank Job"
#93    "Dogs, Dogs, Dogs"
#179   "Wyatt Earp Rides Again"
#188   "The Battle of Mayberry"
#222   "Howard's Main Event"
       All of the above episodes either mention or show the
       Mayberry Grand Theater.

❖  The Cinema Theater is the location for the Annual Meeting of the members of *The Andy Griffith Show* Rerun Watchers Club. This takes place during "Mayberry Days," which are held in Mount Airy, N.C. the last weekend in September each year.

More information on "Mayberry Days" can be found in Section Six.

# An Appeal To The Farmers!

## SWAP TOBACCO FOR PLANES and BOMBS

Idol of the Chinese

COL. VANCE HAYNES

### The PLAN:

Yes, you can swap tobacco for planes and bombs so our own Col. Vance Haynes can carry on his war against the Japs. Just bring a hand or arm of tobacco to the FIRST NATIONAL BANK and it will be kept until the end of the China Relief Campaign and sold on the Mount Airy tobacco market, with the proceeds going to the China Re-

lief Fund which is dedicated to Col. Haynes.

Farmers from Surry and surrounding counties are invited to bring in their tobacco and their names will be recorded in a register to be presented to Col. Haynes. Names of contributors will be published in the newspapers.

**BRING YOUR TOBACCO IN TODAY...LET'S START OFF WITH A BIG PILE**

The tobacco will be stacked in baskets in the lobby of our bank. Help swell the pile with a bunch from your barn. Don't wait until the market opens, but bring it in today and show the na-

tion we are behind our own county boy, Col. Vance Haynes. He is doing a wonderful job directing the airplane attacks against the Japs and we should do our part to support him.

**WATCH THE TOBACCO PILE GROW...HELP IT GROW!**

The author as a Junior WAC

$10,000 FINE AND A YEAR IN PRISON IS THE PENALTY IMPOSED ON ANY PERSON PUTTING CUFFS ON NEW OR WORN WOOL PANTS.

Help FIGHT the war? with the money you save. Buy U.S. WAR BONDS

DRY CLEANING MADE MY OUTFIT AS GOOD AS NEW!

## Hutchens Cleaners Helps You Spend Less To Buy More Defense Bonds

Here's your chance to be patriotic: to forego buying a new outfit this Spring and add more bonds to your defense savings. Send last year's outfit to us. Our modern equipment and careful cleaning services enable us to make it look like new again. And don't forget we can put new life into accessories.

**DO IT NOW BEFORE THE RUSH**

# Hutchens Cleaners

Spring Street                    Phone 688

# 5 | A Big War Comes to a Small Town

IT WAS THE WINTER OF 1941, and the residents of Mount Airy were enjoying that wonderful period between Thanksgiving and Christmas, filled with cooking, baking, and anticipating presents. But on Sunday, December 7th, fear replaced festivities. World War II took center stage in America, and it was the center of attention in Mount Airy as well.

Love of country was one of the basic values I had been taught by my grandparents, Anderson Edward and Ellen Creed. They were very patriotic people, but the idea of another war greatly upset the whole family.

"I don't understand it. After all Grady and the others sacrificed last time, how could it happen again?" The distress in Grandmother's voice was reflected on Grandfather's face.

Mother's older brother, Grady, had been in a world war many years ago that was supposed to end all wars. Lying about his age, he enlisted in the Army at sixteen. He developed tuberculosis while serving overseas, and had spent many months in Veterans Hospitals as a result.

Now another war was taking the best and the brightest youths away from home. I could hear the sadness in the adults' voices as they discussed the day's report from the battle zones. The front page of *The Mount Airy News* was covered with pictures of the area's young men, now in service, with information as to when they were last heard from. Unfortunately, in many cases, the report was that they were missing in action or reported as casualties of battle.

Family prayers at the dinner table now included a blessing for "our men in uniform," and asking God to protect them, so that they would come home safely.

But there were occasions for unity and celebration. A great deal of pride was in the voices of residents when the conversation turned to a local man, Colonel Vance Haynes. He had been made the Director of Bombing Operations for the Allies in China to help protect them from Japanese invasion.

A China Relief drive with many fund-raising activities, was started by the Mount Airy Kiwanis Club and local officials to raise money to assist the Chinese citizens, and also provide Colonel Haynes with needed military supplies and equipment. Local tobacco growers donated portions of their crops to be sold, with the proceeds going to the China Project. The movement spread throughout the state of North Carolina, with an expanded goal of raising enough money to buy a bomber for Colonel Vance Haynes to be used to prevent Japanese invasion of China.

Each Sunday at Central Methodist Church, I heard the minister read the names of the young men who had gone off to help the cause, followed by prayers said for their safe return. Mother joined the rest of the members of the Women's Circles baking cookies, while we, their daughters, proudly packed the goodies in tins for shipment overseas.

I was very proud of the large "V" in the front window. It meant that our family, like many others, had signed a Victory Pledge. Signing that pledge meant that we were committed to strong participation in the war effort, including planting a Victory Garden. Although my grandparents lived on Church Street in the middle of Mount Airy, they already grew many fruits and vegetables in their exceptionally large back yard. During the war they doubled the number of rows of corn, beans, tomatoes, and squash, producing an extra large Victory Garden. They made sure that apples and pears from the many trees on the property were passed on to help those without similar resources. Grandmother also strongly encouraged the tenant farmers on her land out in the country to take pride in planting extra crops for the war effort.

As World War II continued, rationing of all kinds was put into place. Sugar was first. Each family had ration books with stamps showing the amount of sugar that could be purchased by paying the going rate, and turning in the stamps to the merchant. Extra stamps were given to those who used sugar to can fruits and vegetables. Grandmother had always canned; her well-stocked underground cellar was packed with jars of beans, squash, and tomatoes, as well as jams and jellies made from the fruit grown on our property. Normally easy-going, she was somewhat touchy about the number of people who had applied for extra sugar.

"I don't think Mrs. Henderson has ever canned a thing in her life, and there she was, bold as can be, signing up for more sugar for canning. It's just not right. How can she live with herself?" Grandmother grumbled.

Her suspicions were apparently well-founded, as the newspaper reported that out of a population of 35,000 in the county, 30,000 had applied for extra sugar for canning.

Other ration books held red stamps for meat and cheese and blue stamps for processed food. The restrictions on meat annoyed some of our neighbors. They complained bitterly that it just wasn't healthy to limit eating meat that way. I noticed with some satisfaction that they didn't have a "V" sticker on their window.

We were lucky that Grandmother's sister, Mary Jane Belton, lived out in the country at Bannertown. She and her family raised hogs, dairy cows and chickens. As long as we could get good ham, pork chops, ribs, and sausage, we didn't miss the occasional beef roast.

The next item to be rationed was coffee, with an allotment that would provide only a cup a day per person. This particular restriction riled my usually patriotic grandfather, who treasured his cup of coffee as if it were gold.

"I know we need to support the war and all, but how do they expect those of us maintaining the effort at home to keep ourselves alert and moving without a reasonable amount of coffee in our bodies?" It was one of the few times I ever heard him grumble about the sacrifices needed because of the conflict.

Substitutes for meat were encouraged. My favorite dinners included just-baked macaroni and cheese or Grandmother's wonderful navy bean soup, with ham hocks and fatback substituting for the large slices of ham we used to eat. A bowl of that bean soup, served with hot corn bread straight from the iron skillet, slathered with fresh-made butter from Aunt Mary Jane, was one of my favorite meals. Grandfather preferred freshly shot rabbit, fried crispy and served with milk gravy. (Frankly I became very hungry writing this paragraph.)

Grandmother joined with other women at the Home Demonstration Kitchen where instructions were given on how to use refrigerator leftovers to make a new meal. I think this may be when meatloaf was invented. If I ever complained about the contents of a meal, Grandmother swiftly reminded me that "Our boys overseas are existing on C-Rations—having to make do with six small cans of food a day, so you'd better be thankful, young lady, for what you've got here!"

My mother, Mabel, had gotten a job with the War Price Administration, better know as the WPA. Their offices administered the ration laws and issued the stamps. Mother brought home lots of stories about people trying to get stamps they weren't entitled to, as well as specific gossip about neighbors and acquaintances. When the two of us were at our apartment, I always enjoyed listening to Mother's stories. We didn't have that much time together, and I was happy that she would share things with me. It made me feel closer to her.

One evening Mother and I were eating supper at my grandparents' house. Servings of freshly-made pear sonka had just been placed on the table when, with a cheerful voice, Mother entered the stream of conversation started by her parents.

"You'll never believe who came in today with a made-up story about how she dropped her ration book down the grating as she was comin' out of Poore's Grocery." Mother took a deep breath and with a big smile started to complete the story, which was obviously leading up to the revelation of the name of the offender.

In the middle of the narrative, Grandfather interrupted her. "Now, now, Mabel—no need to tell tales out of school." Grandmother nodded her head in agreement. "There'll always be someone that'll try to take advantage of the system, but I reckon I'd just as soon not know exactly who it is."

"But Papa, I'm not telling anything but the truth," Mother declared, straightening herself up to her full 4'10" height.

"That may be so, Mabel, but there are some truths better left unsaid." Grandfather's tone of voice left no doubt that his was expected to be the last word on the matter.

⚜ ⚜

When gasoline rationing went into effect, each person had to prove the necessity of using his or her car in order to get extra gasoline. Each car was required to prominently display a sticker indicating the amount of gasoline allotted. Mother's 1936 Plymouth carried the standard "A" sticker, good for 2880 miles a year, or a little over 55 miles a week. The family Packard also had an "A" sticker, but Grandfather had a "C" sticker, the most liberal amount, for the Model A which he used for business. As United States Marshal and Justice of the Peace, he ranked with doctors and ministers as those whose occupational driving was considered essential.

Grandfather was very careful not to abuse this privilege. I usually went with him as he went about the county attending to his duties. I would sit in the car and read or color until he was finished; then he'd take me for ice cream or a lollipop. All that stopped when gas rationing came in.

"Jewell, I'm sorry. I'd like to take you with me, but people might think we were out pleasure riding. I don't want to give the wrong impression. You understand, don't you, honey?" There was sadness and regret in Grandfather's voice.

I did understand, but I missed those trips so very much. When we used to drive from place to place, Grandfather would talk with me about so many wonderful things. Vital life information was passed on to me that, even today, remains deep in my heart. But I was a proud member of a V-Family, and this was part of my sacrifice for the war effort.

At Rockford Street Grammar School, it was emphasized daily how important it was for all of the children to help collect items needed for the war. Tinfoil was one of the things easy to save. As each piece of gum was unwrapped, I would separate the tinfoil from the paper, smooth it out and put it in the empty round Quaker oatmeal box in the kitchen marked for that purpose. When the box was full, I would proudly take it to school to be added to my schoolmates' collections.

Even though I joined with the rest of the family in their commitment to the war effort, one of the things I tried to get out of doing was the messy job of saving grease. No such luck. Grandmother would always catch me before I could sneak out after dinner.

"Come on young'un, let's get to it. No use puttin' it off. It's gotta be done." It was one of Grandmother's favorite speeches and I had heard it often. "Sing along with the radio; it'll make it easier." She'd go to the Philco radio sitting on the kitchen sideboard and tune it to a station that was playing patriotic music to give us the proper atmosphere.

After each meal the left-over cooking grease was poured through a wire sieve into a large Maxwell House Coffee can. Grandmother would hold the heavy cast iron skillet over the can, pouring the grease. My job was to use a large wooden spoon to remove the left-over food scrapings from the wire mesh basket so that the grease going into the can was as pure as possible. When the grease in the can weighed a pound or more, Grandmother would give it to Grandfather and me to take to the Sanitary Meat Market. The folks there would give us two red stamps for each pound and then send it on to the government collection point, where it would be transferred to a central collection station for the state.

☙ ❧

During the war, there was a great deal of emphasis on the importance of not wasting anything. All the children in our neighborhood kept on the lookout for scrap metal. We would take anything we found to the basement of the school and put it in a special barrel. Each grade would compete to see who could bring in the most pounds of metal. On Saturdays the Center Theater gave free admission to children who brought in scrap rubber. I always tried to find enough to get in to see the latest Hopalong Cassidy movie.

☙ ❧

On my eighth birthday, Grandfather bought a $25 War Bond in my name. At school, the members of each class brought in change to buy savings stamps for 25¢ each. When a stamp book was filled with $18.75 worth of stamps, it could be exchanged for a War Bond that would pay back $25 when it matured in ten years. Ads in the paper encouraged buying as many bonds as possible to raise the money needed to build guns, tanks, and planes.

☙ ❧

Even politics was affected by the war. One of the men who was running for Clerk of the Court withdrew his name from the race, explaining, "Conditions have developed since my entering the race that would make it necessary for me to spend some money to make a campaign. I do not have the funds, because within a few days after the attack on Pearl Harbor, I invested what I could in War Bonds. I greatly appreciate the efforts of my friends in my behalf, but having two sons in the military, I have decided that all the efforts of our people during these critical days should be expended in the effort to win the war."

☙ ❧

Even though we lived a good ways inland from the Atlantic Ocean, we were still concerned about enemy attacks. The first time I heard the new sound of airplanes overhead, I was scared, as were many of the town's residents who sought shelter in their houses and shops. Fortunately, a Winston-Salem radio station quickly identified the planes as being those of the US Army Air Force on their way to a base in Georgia.

As I look back to those days, I realize what extraordinary times they were. In the process of uniting the nation to support the effort to preserve our nation and way of life, families and communities were brought together in ways they had never experienced before. I wish we could have that experience again—not to protect ourselves from enemies from without—but to achieve a common goal of greatness within.

## TAGS *Notes:*

Episode

#6      "Ellie Comes to Town"
        Andy was said to be in Paris, France during WWII

#8      "A Feud Is a Feud"
        Reference is again made to Andy's having been in France during the WWII, and that he learned a few words of French while he was there.

#29     "Quiet Sam"
        Barney says that he served in the Army during WWII. He was responsible for more than 3,000 books at the Post Exchange on Staten Island. When pressed for details, Barney said he'd "rather not talk about it."

#82     "Class Reunion"
        The high school yearbook indicates that Barney was on the Board of Directors for the tinfoil drive.

#136  "Opie's Fortune"
Mentions Bannertown, a real village just outside Mount Airy.

❖ As many of the devoted watchers of TAGS have learned, there were many "discrepancies" in the "facts" given on the show. Some of the more obvious ones are in connection with World War II. Both Andy and Barney are in the same class at Mayberry High and graduate in 1945— or 1948 as given in Episode #176.

❖ The United States came into World War II after the bombing of Pearl Harbor on December 7, 1941. WWII ended in August of 1945 with the cessation of combat in the Pacific Theater.

If Andy and Barney were graduating from high school in either 1945 or 1948, Barney could hardly have been assigned to WWII duty at the Post exchange in Staten Island during the war. By the same token, Andy would not have been assigned to duty in France during that period.

❖ Andy Griffith actually graduated from Mount Airy High School in June of 1944.

❖ Colonel Vance Haynes became a Brigadier General before the end of the war. Col. Haynes was the grandson of Chang Bunker, one of the Siamese Twins. See Section Three for the story of The Siamese Twins, who lived many years in the Mount Airy area.

# 6 | Riding the Radio Waves

IT IS HARD TO OVERSTATE THE IMPORTANCE of radio in my early life. Would I have received such a broad knowledge of world events if I hadn't listened to "Dr. I. Q.," "Information Please," and "The Quiz Kids," regularly? What if I hadn't heard Gabriel Heater's news broadcasts every night with my mother, or sat at my Grandfather's feet as he gave full attention to President Roosevelt's "Fireside Chats"? And my ability to recall the names of both famous and obscure songs—how much of that gift may be due to NBC's "Kay Kaiser's Kollege of Musical Knowledge" each Wednesday night, and "Your Hit Parade" every Saturday night? I was raised to value information, and in those days, most of our information came from the ever-present radio.

If there had been an Arbitron tracking organization for radio usage in the 1930's and 1940's, I'm sure my grandparents' household would have been a prized one. There were radios everywhere. A four-foot high Philco floor model was in the parlor: a very formal-looking cherry-wood radio, suited to the decor of the room, which was only used on Sundays and special occasions. The dining room sported a smaller RCA table-top model—strategically placed so that a number of chairs could be pulled around it to facilitate

easy listening and viewing. Yes, viewing! Today's television generation may find it hard to visualize three adults and a child in a semi-
circle around a radio so that they could all clearly *see* the source of
the entertaining sounds coming into the room.

Both the master bedroom upstairs and one bedroom downstairs
sported tabletop models, and there was a small white plastic radio
on the kitchen counter. "Might as well listen to 'Our Gal Sunday'
while making lunch," Grandmother would say. "It'll make the time
go faster."

Let's see now—that would add up to five radios at their
house—and I had gotten a new style "portable" one for my birthday; plus mother and I had two more radios in the Snyder Court
Apartments where we lived. Yes, the radio certainly played an important part in our lives.

On Sunday evenings, the RCA in my grandparents' dining room
was the focus of our listening pleasure. After the round cherry
dining table had been cleared of supper dishes, it would be reset
with pastel linen place mats which my grandmother had enhanced
with hand-tatted edges. Pear pie, or some other delicious homemade dessert, would be served, accompanied by our favorite beverages. Coffee for Grandfather and Mother; hot tea for Grandmother; and hot chocolate or a glass of sweet milk for me.

What wonderful times they were! I would sit close to Grandfather, sometimes climbing into his lap after he finished his cigar. I
adored my grandfather. My mother and father had separated when I
was 3 years old, and Grandfather had provided a much-needed
male influence in my life. He talked to me as an adult, and every
day taught me some new and wonderful thing about the world.

Once 6:30 PM came and it was time for "The Great
Gildersleeve," attentive listening became the order of the evening. I
didn't really understand much of that program, but so enjoyed being included with the adults that I made no mention of any questions I might have had.

At 7 o'clock Grandfather would change the dial to the NBC
station for "The Jack Benny Show." Grandfather especially enjoyed
Jack Benny. Every week he would mention that Jack's penny-pinch-
ing ways reminded him of Grandmother, and every week she would

challenge his assessment of what she felt was her appropriately thrifty nature.

"Now Ed, if I didn't look out for the pennies, we wouldn't have any dollars. You'd give 'em all away 'helping' other people. I'm the one who has to make sure we have something left for us to live on!"

She always sounded peeved, but I knew better. So many times I had seen her give clothes and food to others, and even take money out of her "secret" jar hidden in the back of the kitchen cabinet to give to someone in need.

We stayed with CBS to listen to "Edgar Bergen & Charlie McCarthy." I was so intrigued by them! I had seen pictures of Charlie and had clear explanations of his wooden nature, but his expressions were so real, I found myself disbelieving the adult explanation of what a "dummy" was. Especially with Charlie teasing Edgar about Edgar's mouth moving when Charlie was talking. How could he do that if he wasn't real?

At 9 o'clock we tuned in Fred Allen and "Allen's Alley," on the ABC station. Grandfather would laugh all the way through the show, with Grandmother and Mother "shushing" him frequently so that they could hear what was being said on the program.

Mother usually took me home to our apartment before "Inner Sanctum" came on. She said it was because she was worried that the squeaking door and all the eerie sound effects would scare me and I wouldn't sleep well. The truth was, it was Mother who was uncomfortable with the images. I liked being somewhat frightened. If it got to be too scary, I could just look over at my Grandfather and I'd feel safe again.

Radio programs were a significant part of my life all during the week. Mother and I ate supper at my grandparents' house most weekdays. I came straight to their house after school, and Mother would join us after she finished work. On Monday nights, Grandmother would delay supper until after "Lum and Abner" came on on NBC at 6:30 PM. It was my grandfather's favorite show. First airing in 1931, it ran for 24 years. One of Grandfather's favorite episodes was "The Insurance Salesman." While it was a very funny program, Grandfather made sure I understood the lesson: that I shouldn't "count my chickens (or insurance policies) before they were hatched."

Mother liked the late afternoon dramatic programs. Her favorite was "The Romance of Helen Trent." In later years those kind of shows came to be known as "soap operas" because the programs were usually sponsored by companies that made laundry products.

I listened to many programs with my mother and grandparents, but the one show that was mine alone came on Saturday morning. It was "Let's Pretend" and showcased wonderful fairy tales. For that half-hour, I was transported to exotic lands and met exciting people. My favorite story was one where a wicked something or other had turned several young men into swans. Their sister tried to break the evil spell by knitting sweaters to cover their wings. Although she worked many days and nights knitting and knitting, she didn't get completely through with all of them and one brother was left with one arm and one wing. I cried every time I heard the story. I was an only child, but if I had any brothers, I was sure I would have worked just as hard for them.

One of the programs Grandmother especially liked was a gospel show broadcast from WBT in Charlotte. A male quartet always opened the show with, "Turn your radio on, and listen to the music in the air. Turn the lights down low, and listen to the Master's radio."

Grandmother and I would sing along with the hymns and gospel songs. As we listened, her fingers kept time to the music as she deftly crocheted some new item for her home. A contented smile on her face, she would say the same thing every week:

"Ya know, honey, the things I make while I listen to God's music are always my best pieces."

Just as today's families have favorite television shows that they make a special effort to see, in my childhood, there were special radio shows that kept us coming back week after week.

One of the dramatic, sing-song, opening lines still rings in my head: "Grand... Cen-tral... Sta-tion—crossroads of a million private lives—a gigantic stage on which are played a thousand dramas daily!"

# TAGS *Notes:*

Episode

#46     "Keeper of the Flame"
        Andy and Opie tease Aunt Bee for listening to soap operas
        on the radio.

#116    "The Song Festers"
        Group sings "Santa Lucia" on YLRB in Mount Pilot.

#128    "Barney's Bloodhound"
        Andy and Barney regularly listen to Leonard Blush and his
        operatic melodies from WMPD in Mount Pilot. (In Episode
        #116 Blush's program is stated as airing every third Tuesday
        from YLRB in Mount Pilot.)

#161    "Opie's Job"
        Norris Goff, who portrayed Abner Peabody on "Lum and
        Abner," appears as the store owner, Mr. Doakes.

❖   As Andy grew up, the main entertainment at the Griffith home
    was listening to the radio. The whole family listened to the
    comedy and drama programs, and Andy sang along with the
    country and gospel music.

❖   One of his father's favorite radio shows was, "The Lone Ranger."
    Andy said his father, Carl, not only listened attentively, but
    joined in with the radio actors in responding to the question,
    "Who was that masked man?"

❖   Many of the wonderful old radio shows are available on cassette
    tape. The *Radio Classics*™ series is available at all the Cracker
    Barrel Country Stores and at their website: www.
    crackerbarrel.com

Doc and Ida

# 7 | *Doc and Ida*

AS LONG AS ANYONE COULD REMEMBER, Doc and Ida were a familiar sight on the streets of Mount Airy. The two were always together and presented a distinctive fashion statement. It appeared that all the clothes they owned were layered on their bodies at any one time. It was a convenient way to keep track of their apparel, since they had no regular dwelling place. Doc wore a crumpled fedora that sat somewhat precariously above his wide forehead. Ida, on the other hand, kept a bell-shaped cloth hat pulled so far down over her head that her eyebrows were barely visible.

In the summers, while they were walking down the streets, as the temperature warmed up, the couple would discard items of clothing until they were comfortable. Thankfully, they always stopped before embarrassing themselves or others. How and when they retrieved the clothes is not certain, but the same garments were seen layered on the couple when the weather turned cold again.

Today, Doc and Ida might be called "homeless people," but while they may not have had a house to live in, they certainly had a home in Mount Airy. Those were more compassionate times, when people looked out after each other. Although the pair was some-times seen foraging through containers of discarded items behind businesses and homes, most of the time the town's merchants ac-tively sought to do what they could to help out the couple. Walter Poore, a local grocer, put aside fruits and vegetables at the end of the day for the couple to pick up. Other merchants made sure that "discards" were offered to the two on a regular basis.

In the summer, Doc and Ida would generally sleep outdoors. In winter, they knew that if the temperature was going to be near freezing, several of the night watchmen at the furniture factories and knitting mills would open their back doors so that the couple could come in quietly and sleep near the furnace.

Although he walked the streets regularly, few people knew the man's real name. The title "Doc" was given to him because of the little black bag he carried constantly. The bag was filled with Doc's personal selection of herbs, plant extracts and oils. He always claimed that the bag contained all he needed to keep himself and his wife well.

Apparently Doc's knowledge of natural remedies was as good as he alleged. The story is told of the time a farmer named Jessup came into town for some provisions. His youngest daughter was quite ill with the measles. When Jessup spied Doc and Ida on the street, he reckoned as how it wouldn't hurt to try a little of Doc's medicine to help his Elva, so he picked up the pair and took them back to the farm.

Doc and Ida proceeded to the kitchen where Doc painstakingly selected an assortment of leaves and herbs and gave them Ida. She carefully placed the mixture in boiling water and brewed a murky-looking tea, mumbling a mysterious incantation as she stirred. The sick child was persuaded to drink the somewhat less than tasty concoction, after which the young girl drifted off to sleep. The farmer returned Doc and his wife to town, expressing his thanks with an assortment of farm fresh food and a couple of blankets.

Later that week, Jessup joined a group of men at their regular morning gathering and gossip session around the pot-bellied stove at Holcomb's Hardware on Main Street.

"How's ya young'un doing?" one of the men inquired.

"I heard tell that you had Doc and Ida come out to ya place."

"I sho nuf did," Jessup answered, "and by cracky, my Elva perked up right away! She was feeling so much better the next day that she asked if she could come out 'n hep me milk the cow. It was nigh on to a miracle!"

"But last year when my Molly had the measles, I brought her into town to see ole Doc Woltz. He was nice enuf all right, but it cost me a purty penny by the time I got the store-bought medicine. And it took Molly near a week to get on her feet. Yessir, next time any of my kin gets sickly, I'm bringing Doc and Ida back to the farm."

Doc and Ida wandered the streets of Mount Airy every day for many years, being seen in many widely separated parts of town. One of their favorite strolls ended at the low granite wall in front of the historic Hadley House on West Pine Street. They would sit in the shade for as long as they liked before continuing their never ending journey. Since many houses had low walls made of Mount Airy granite, there were a number of places they could rest along the way. Occasionally, word would circulate that they had been seen in Toast, Dobson or Pilot Mountain, apparently the beneficiaries of a ride in someone's car. But always, they would return to their "home"—the streets of Mount Airy.

George W. Jackson, aka "Doc" died in 1947 at the age of 88 after age and infirmity had put both him and Ida in residence at the County Home. His death brought out some previously unknown relatives of Ida, who took her out of the Home and, from all accounts, worked wonders with both her physical looks and the use of her mental capacities. She lived to be 92, resided in an apartment of her own, and attended church regularly. Ida still depended on others for rides, but now she had one or two special people who helped her to get around, and whom she regarded as friends.

It was reported that Doc and Ida walked and lived on the streets of the area for about 50 years. There is no record of their having encountered any harassment, assault, robbery or suffering at the hands of others.

❖ A recurring theme in the episodes of *The Andy Griffith Show* was the caring and compassion of the townspeople toward residents and strangers alike. This attitude echoes the atmosphere in Mount Airy as Andy was growing up.

# Where's Barney When You Need Him?

"It's a wilderness out there. And every so often a beast of prey comes sneaking in. Now it's my job as a lawman to stalk him and run him out. You just never know when another beast might come down out of the forest."

"You know, Andy, I never thought our town would come to this. Mayberry—Gateway to Danger."

— Deputy Barney Fife

# County Jail Chix Roost Is Raided

## Glenn Monday and Hoffman Wells Try To Make Way With Jailer Monday's Supply.

The prize could well be awarded Glenn Monday of this city for sheer audacity and reckless disregard of the usual care observed by the criminal to avoid capture and imprisonment when he raided the poultry yard of his cousin, Jailer J. E. Monday at the county jail in Dobson about three o'clock Thursday morning. He had parked his car right at the door of the jail as if he expected to break into jail, which it later amounted to, and in company with Hoffman Wells the two proceeded to sack up the chickens on the roost at the back of the jail.

Mr. Monday heard the commotion in the yard and on looking out the window saw Wells coming across the yard with a sack full of chickens slung across his shoulders. Mr. Monday was undressed and hurried out, not taking time to put on any sox or shoes. Wells took adantage of the officer by taking off down through the fields where briars and brambles are thickest, and the first few steps taken by the officer filled his feet full of briars and he gave up the chase. Turning back to the jail yard he found his cousin Glenn Monday, trying to get a car started and Mr. Monday captured him before he could make his escape.

In the car was found two other sacks of chickens which had been taken off the roost of some farmer, but their ownership has not been ascertained by the officers.

Wells succeeded in eluding capture but Monday was lodged in Dobson jail. It is recalled that these two men some weeks ago were bound to the Superior Court on a charge of highway robbery, it being alleged they robbed Cecil Gates near this city of his money and clothes as they were taking Gates to his home near the foot of the mountain. Later the two gave bond on the robbery charge and were released from jail until their trial in October

# "Petting Parties" Held At Cemetery

## Officers To Arrest Offenders For Trespassing.

Those folks who have been using the grounds of Oakdale Cemetery for "petting parties" are warned by the officers that they stand in danger of being arrested and brought into court on charges of trespass. Sheriff Thompson and Chief Lawrence have been appealed to in the prevention of this practice at the cemetery and they are warning such offenders that trespass of the property will be prosecuted in the courts.

Its the plan of the officers to patrol the grounds at various intervals and anyone guilty of trespassing on the property will be arrested and brought into court.

Never before has it been necessary to take such action for the protection of the cemetery but the officers say the condition has become a nuisance and they expect to break it up.

# 8 | *Give Me Just One Good Deputy*

*"You looked over all the candidates, you judged their qualifications and their character and their ability, and you come to the fair, the just, and the honest conclusion that I was the best-suited for the job. And I want to thank you, cousin Andy."*
—Deputy Barney Fife

TRULY, DEPUTY BARNEY FIFE was an exceptional man. He was the only deputy that Sheriff Andy Taylor needed to handle the day-to-day operations of all of Mayberry County and keep its residents safe and secure. Deputy Fife was so committed to making sure all the roads in outlying areas were safe, he bought a World War I motorcycle and sidecar at a war surplus auction in Mount Pilot, just so he could be on duty when Andy was using the patrol car. Yes-siree, all 4,000 inhabitants of the area slept well at night, knowing that Andy and Barney were on the job.

By way of contrast, shortly after Sheriff Sam Patterson took office in Surry County, North Carolina in 1942, he assessed the needs of the 6,000 residents of the county and immediately appointed 20 men as Deputy Sheriffs to fan out over the area. Mount Airy, Bryan, Dobson, Elkin, Bannertown, Toast, Rockford, Pinnacle, Lowgap, Siloam, Shoals, Stewarts Creek, Westfield, Eldora, Ararat, Rural Hall; all would have their own special deputies.

Of course, knowing Sheriff Sam's habit of keeping in touch with the people, it was good public and political relations to have uniformed officers in as many places as possible. In addition, the fees received for serving official papers probably helped the officers' families keep food on the table.

What a delight to know that Sheriff Sam needed all those deputies, while Sheriff Andy got the job done with the one and only Barney.

As Deputy Barney Fife would have put it, "My job is "Big, Really Big!"

## TAGS *Notes:*

Episode

#112   "Barney's Sidecar"

# 9 | *Handling Serious Lawbreakers*

"WELL, BOYS, WHAT ARE WE GONNA DO? This situation is gettin' way out of hand. I'm afraid we're gonna have to take action soon!" Chief of Police Lawrence's tone of voice underscored his concern about the seriousness of the situation.

"But Chief, ya know we can't pick up all of 'em that are breakin' the law. We ain't got enuf cells to hold 'em," one of the policemen chimed in. His opinion was underscored by a chorus of "That's for sure," and "Amen, brother," from the others present at the meeting.

"You're right," the Chief agreed, " 'cause it ain't just the young people that are doin' it. We'd be pickin' up lawyers, bankers, and some of the City Councilmen, and that wouldn't set too well with any of 'em."

After a lot of jawing amongst the men, the Chief decided on a plan: target the young people first; get the word out that there will be increased vigilance by law enforcement; and issue a strong warning to stop the dreaded activities.

Next Friday's issue of *The Mount Airy News* carried the bold headline:

"OFFICERS TO CURB
DOUBLE PARKING EVIL."

The Chief used the newspaper article to appeal to the citizens of the city to "show a better observance of the parking laws."

"Why, visitors are telling me that they find it more difficult to get through the streets of Mount Airy than they do in most any large city!"

Chief Lawrence acknowledged that it would be very upsetting to everyone if they started out tomorrow to arrest every citizen found guilty of violating the parking laws. However, he insisted, "This situation just can't be allowed to continue."

According to the report, contributing significantly to the problem were the groups of young people who were driving up to the drug stores, and calling for ice cream and soda to be brought out to them. They remained double parked while the order was prepared and brought to the car.

Then, once they had their drinks and ice cream, they continued to stay in the same spot for another 15 minutes or so while they enjoyed their treats, creating a menace to the through traffic on the street.

"This has got to stop!" the Chief insisted, adding that the enforcement of all traffic regulations is an unpleasant duty for the officers and requires the cooperation of the citizens of the city to make it effective.

Chief Lawrence ended his appeal by reporting that he had discussed the situation with the Main Street merchants, and had received their assurance that they will cooperate by "refusing to serve customers who are double parked on the street!"

The newspaper article ended by making a final plea with the citizens to help  STOP THIS DOUBLE PARKING EVIL!

# TAGS *Notes:*

Episode

#148　"Barney Runs For Sheriff"
　　　In his speech Barney says that the traffic in Mayberry is "out of control."

#186　"Goober's Replacement"
　　　Sheriff Taylor mentions that Weavers Department Store has a problem with double parking.

# 10 | Thumbs Up!

IT WAS NEAR MIDNIGHT WHEN a passing motorist spotted the two boys standing on the side of the road that led from Mount Airy to Pilot Mountain and then on to Winston-Salem. Kind of late for boys who looked to be no more than 14 or 15 years old to be on the highway, he thought, slowing his car with the idea of stopping to see if they needed help of any kind. As his car came closer, his headlights illuminated the boys' hands piled high with shiny pocket knives. Wait a minute, he thought, that don't look right. I'll better tell somebody about it. Down the road apiece, the man pulled into a filling station and asked the owner if he could use his phone.

Back in Mount Airy, Policeman C. F. Melton had checked out the police station one last time and was locking up when the phone rang. "Now who's that calling at this hour?" he wondered out loud. "My shift's up and I'm ready to go home." But even as he said it, he knew in this small town there was never a time when he was really off-duty. With a sigh, he turned back to the desk and answered the phone.

Melton hung the receiver up quickly, then took his policeman's cap off his head and replaced it with an old fedora that had been left at the station weeks ago. He took a plain brown cotton jacket from the rickety coat rack, put it on over his uniform, and buttoned it up. Locking the station door quickly, Melton got into his personal 1936 green Plymouth, mashed down the gas pedal and "scratched off" up Monroe Street, then turned left onto Main. There were no other cars on the road so he was half-way to Pilot Mountain in jig time.

It didn't take long to spot the boys. There they were, near the top of Boone's hill, a pair of thumbs extended in the universally accepted "please pick me up" sign. As the officer pulled to a stop, his headlights shone on two young men whose trouser pockets were bulging significantly.

"Need a lift, guys?"

"Yes-sah, we'd sho 'preciate it," the taller of the two responded.

"Well climb on in," Melton invited, and the boys stepped onto the running board and then into the car.

The two settled down in the back seat and began to talk softly to each other. They were so engrossed in conversation that Melton made a U-turn and started back toward town before the boys noticed what was happening.

"S'cuse me sir—we thawt you'd be goin' to Winston-Salem."

"Got sumpin' I need to take care of in Mount Airy first. You boys don't mind the ride, do ya?"

"Guess not," the first boy said, reluctantly.

The three rode in silence until Policeman Melton made the turn onto Monroe Street and pulled the car up in front of the Police Station and Jail. He got out of the car and opened the back door to find two very frightened boys slumped down in the back seat.

In the Station, the contents of their pockets were being inventoried as the phone rang.

"Yessah, Mr. Midkiff, I know your hardware store was broken into. Yeas, I know someone took 29 new pocket knives, two watches and, I believe, sumpin' like nine dollars and eight cents."

There was a pause, and then Policeman Melton continued, with more than a trace of pride in his voice.

"When we say the Mount Airy Police Department is always on the job, we mean it, sir. I've not only got your property back, I got the two boys that did it. Got 'em in custody right here now."

"And what's more," he continued with a smile and a laugh, "I did a good deed tonight. I gave two young hitch-hikers the ride they deserved."

## TAGS *Notes:*

Episode

#117  "The Shoplifters"
      "Weavers Department Store is losing merchandise. Barney to the rescue!

#178  "Lost and Found"
      Aunt Bee declares that "Andy wouldn't let any thieves be in Mayberry."

"Well, I guess to sum it up, you could say there's three reasons why there's so little crime in Mayberry. There's Andy, and there's me, and (patting his gun) "baby" makes three."

—Deputy Barney Fife

# 11 | *If At First You Don't Succeed*

BACK IN THE SPRING OF 1943, a local 16 year-old named Edgar did his best to be a one-boy crime streak, but never could get the process quite right. He had a hankerin' for automobiles and tried out quite a few.

First was Mr. Wilson Barber's car, which Edgar took on April 2nd and drove until the gas gave out. A week later on April 9th, he took a fancy to Zeb Martin's car, and stole it from in front of Mr. Martin's house on Church Street, driving the car 45 miles down the road to Winston-Salem before it gave out of gas.

Martin had alerted the police, and the young man was picked up in Winston-Salem and brought back to Mount Airy to enjoy the hospitality of the City Jail. Edgar wasn't particularly pleased with the prospect, and managed to get away from the officers and escape from the lobby of the jail.

One might think the youth would get as far away from the jail as possible, but not this boy; the next night officers caught him sleeping in the hay back of C. G. Lovill's place of business, not two blocks away. They immediately apprehended him and placed him in jail, making sure he was securely held-on-to in the process.

There was lots of finger-pointing between the officers when Edgar's cell was found empty only two days later. He had managed to saw out the bars on his cell and make his getaway to parts unknown.

Two more days passed until the 14th, when the young man stole Bill Miller's pick-up truck from Virginia Street. Bill had just filled the truck up at Bray's Esso Station, so the youth managed to drive the truck to Wilkesboro before it ran out of gas. There he stole a tank of fuel and made his way back to Elkin on the 15th until once more the fuel gave out. Edgar couldn't find a way to steal gas in Elkin, so he opted for taking another car and drove it to Dobson. When it sputtered to a stop, he abandoned it.

On the same day, the elusive Edgar hitchhiked to White Plains where he took another car and drove it until its tank was empty. Officers spotted him as he was attempting to steal gas once more, but he fled as they approached. They later found him hiding in the basement of an apartment on Pine Street, and finally were able to bring him back to jail, where he remained until his court hearing.

It was discovered that during the same period, the energetic delinquent, with the help of other younger boys, had broken into the Center Theater and stolen $600 in tickets, as well as being responsible for the breakage of 40 window panes at a grammar school.

Guess we have to give Edgar credit for being focused on what he wanted and fearless in its pursuit. Or as my Grandmother Creed used to say:

"Might as well give the devil his due."

## TAGS *Notes:*

Episode

#164  "Malcolm at the Crossroads"
Ernest T. Bass gets out of jail several times without anyone being able to figure out how he did it.

# 12 | Nude Rider

THE STORY SPREAD IN HUSHED WHISPERS, accompanied by subdued giggles, as it took over the conversation at the monthly meeting of the United Daughters of the Confederacy.

"Is it true that Margaret Anne actually saw him?" The plump lady in the pink suit delivered her inquiry in a voice that seemed both shocked and intrigued.

"Well, if he came to *my* house looking like that, I certainly wouldn't look at him!" A woman dressed all in navy blue spoke forcefully, pulling her wide-brimmed straw hat down in front of her eyes to accentuate her point.

The first report had come in several weeks ago from a local filling station. A car drove up and the attendant came out, and started toward the driver's window to see how many gallons of gas the customer wanted to buy. As he approached, the driver called out, "fill 'er up."

The attendant filled up car with the gasoline and returned to the driver to get the money for the transaction. "That'll be $4." The driver handed him the correct amount and drove away. It was an ordinary transaction except for one thing. The young man driving the car was *stark naked*!

There were similar occurrences at other filling stations and the police had been on alert to try to catch the offender.

The ribald situation had been the topic of much conversation in Mount Airy for several weeks. At the City Barber Shop, the men waiting for haircuts put in their two-cents-worth.

"Sho' wonder who it is. Chester over at the fillin' station said he didn't recognize him, and he knows everybody."

"Waal, ya know Chester; he might not 'a been lookin' at the man's face!

Hearty laughter followed and set off a round of half-whispered stories.

For the last thirty days all the law enforcement officers in Surry and adjacent counties had been searching for the young man, to no avail. However, when reports of a new, even more shocking episode reached them, they stepped up their efforts.

It seemed that in the middle of the afternoon the young man stopped his car in front of Mrs. Rastus Gilley's house. He proceeded to get out of the automobile and in the presence of her daughter and a visiting girl, presented himself totally devoid of clothing. Mrs. Gilley quickly sent the young girls into the house and boldly confronted the young man.

"How dare you show yourself this way, and in front of impressionable young girls to boot. I'm calling the Sheriff about you right this minute!" She turned and went quickly into the house. The young man was seen calmly getting back into his car and driving off.

There were many other complaints and finally, based upon a number of descriptions of the car, the suspect was apprehended and found to be a resident of the Winston-Salem area. The officers were surprised to learn that he was the son of a prominent and well-regarded family.

The suspect, Oscar, was brought before Judge H. H. Llewellyn, who found him guilty and sentenced him to one year on the road crew. However, the Judge offered to dismiss the sentence if Oscar's parents would be willing to take the young man in charge and have him put in a mental institution for observation. The parents angrily refused the offer. Oscar's father made his feelings very clear.

"No way am I going to accept a sentence coming from a small judge in a small town! I am formally requesting a jury trial at the county seat."

At the trial at the Dobson County Courthouse the young man's family brought many friends and relatives to speak in behalf of Oscar. In addition, his father had gathered a host of prominent witnesses from Winston-Salem to testify to his son's good character.

When the presiding judge mentioned that some of the Sheriff's deputies had complained that Oscar's father had accosted them in the hall of the Courthouse, and made what could be interpreted as threats against them, it set the man off even more. Jumping to his feet in the courtroom where all, including the jury could hear, he exclaimed:

"Don't know what y'all are trying to prove in this backwoods court. This ridiculous arrest would never have happened in Winston-Salem!"

It required the jury less than a half-hour to return to court with a verdict of "guilty." Oscar was fined $500, plus court costs of $217. He received probation, with the condition that he was to remain in good behavior for five years, or face 12 months of road work.

It is not known whether or not Oscar caused any similar trouble elsewhere, but he never returned to Mount Airy, and for good reason.

As the President of the Womens' Garden Club announced at their first meeting after the trial:

"We just don't tolerate that kind of thing in Mount Airy!"

# The Mount Airy News
Classified Ads - One cent per word with 25¢ minimum
1930's and 1940's

---

LOST OR STRAYED — 2 Pigs about 6 weeks old, color white and black. If you have information of their where abouts see or write Mrs. W. L. Chilton, Ararat, N. C.

---

FOR SALE — 4 Tennessee Walking Horses. Gentle and lady broke. Aged 4 and 5 years old. See C. W. Fulton. Mount Airy, N.C.

---

KEEP YOUR WIFE for a pet and buy lunch at The Canteen Bigger and Better than ever. Jim Barker and Lee Dunman.

---

WANTED TO BUY Kitchen fats. tallow oils, any kind usable to make soap. Will pay 5 cents pound. I handle. J. R. Watkins products

---

REWARD — $5 reward for information as to who ran into picket fence on Rockford street March 7 with a blue car, driver looked to be a mechanic. Mrs. C. W. Davis.

---

BACHELOR WANTS WIFE — Between age of 16 and 45 years. Good character and health required. Photo requested with answer. C. W. Jackson, Mount Airy, N. C. Route 1, Box 39

---

FOR SALE — House and lot East Oak Street. 4 rooms, bath, garage, convenient location. Bargain price $1200 Terms. J. Will Prather

---

STRAY HOG — A Sow hog, weight 125 lbs. strayed from its owner is now at my home. Owner can get same by calling and paying cost I have been put to. V. L. Simmons, City. R.I

---

BABY AND STARTED CHICKS — We have plenty of heavy and light breeds and now is the time to start your winter layers to avoid any molt. All blood tested and fumigated. Mount Airy Hatchery, Mount Airy, N.C.

# Believe It Or Not!

## IT'S THE LAW!

The first printed laws of the town of Mount Airy after its incorporation in 1885 included the following:

NO person shall drive or back his wagon upon any public sidewalk of the town for the purpose of loading or unloading goods unless by permission of the Mayor.

NO one shall drive a horse, mule or cow along the sidewalks of the town or hitch same to any fence or shade tree.

NO person shall obstruct the sidewalks or streets by playing marbles, or by playing ball, or by pitching quoits thereon.

NO wood, coal, chips or trash accumulating from cutting wood shall be permitted to remain on Main Street for a longer period than 12 hours, under penalty of one dollar.

ANY person who shall roll, or cause to be rolled, any hogshead or barrel of any sort upon the streets and sidewalks of Mount Airy, in view of any horse or horses or mules in the streets, shall pay one dollar for the offense.

HOTEL porters and all persons soliciting travel for hotels, boarding houses and at the trains, shall confine themselves to the platform on the east side of the depot. Crowding around the cars or reception rooms on the arrival of trains in such manner as to interfere with the business of the employees of the railroad, or of the free access of passengers to and from trains is declared a nuisance. Every violator shall be fined $10.

IT SHALL be the duty of the Police to impound all hogs running at large and sell them after three days notice.

THE shooting of shot or other missles from rubbers or bean shooters upon the streets is declared a nuisance and parties convicted will be fined one dollar. Parents are responsible for minors.

A TAX of 33 1-3 cents on real estate and personal property is levied, and one dollar on every pole.

Eng and Chang Bunker
The Original Siamese Twins

*Photo courtesy of the Mount Airy Visitors Information Center*

# 13 | *The Siamese Twins*

THE STRIKING LITHOGRAPH WAS DISPLAYED prominently
on the wall of the entrance hall of my grandparents' home on
Church Street: two men with oriental features, dressed formally in
three-piece suits, shiny black shoes, white shirts with black bow
ties at the neck.

As a little girl, I was fascinated by the picture. I never tired of
my grandfather telling me the story of Eng and Chang Bunker, who
had come to be known around the world as the "Siamese Twins."

"They're buried right up the road apiece," he'd say, always start-
ing at the end of their story, not the beginning. "They were good
men, and good citizens, and we're lucky they decided to settle in
this area."

I was about 5 years old when I first asked my grandfather about
the picture. It was not what they were wearing that I noticed first. It
was the five-inch wide band of flesh at their chests joining them
together.

I remember giggling as I pointed to the picture:

"They look so strange with that funny-looking piece of skin
between them. How in the world do they walk around and do
things, when they're hooked up like that?"

A frown crossed my grandfather's face, and his voice became uncommonly stern. "Now Jewell, it's not right to laugh at people just because they look different. God created *all* of us. Those two young men just happened to be born that way. They never knew anything else, so they found ways of making the best of the situation. I imagine they went through a lot because of ignorant people makin' fun of them."

His rebuke worried me. The last thing I wanted was for my beloved grandfather to be disappointed in me.

"I'm sorry. I shouldn't have laughed at them. I know they couldn't help how they looked."

Grandfather's voice softened as he continued. "Just because they looked different, some people called them 'freaks' and were afraid to be around them. The truth was, they were both intelligent, caring individuals and deserved to be accepted as regular men. Fortunately, the people in this area accepted them as they were, and that is one of the reasons they settled here."

Grandfather continued with the lesson. "The most important thing the Siamese Twins can teach us is that people should be accepted for what's *inside* them, not how they look on the outside." From his tone of voice I knew he expected me to remember his words and act accordingly.

Over the years Grandfather used the picture of the Twins for additional valuable lessons. One of the attributes of the Twins that impressed him most had been their keen intellect and knowledge on many subjects. Although they had never had any formal schooling, they had learned how to read and write and could easily converse on many subjects. They were also good businessmen, and had a reputation for being able to negotiate as good a bargain as anyone.

"Remember, Jewell, what you learn in school - why that's just the beginning of your education. Read everything you can; listen to those that are older and wiser than you; be curious; be open to new ideas. That's what real wisdom is all about, and honey, it's out there for anybody that takes the time to learn it."

✤ ✤

Much information and misinformation has been written about Eng and Chang Bunker, the "Siamese Twins." Recent years have seen both non-fiction and fiction books on their lives, as well as a play and a musical.

The Twins were born on a bamboo mat in a houseboat near Bangkok in 1811. As they grew up, they helped their widowed mother in the duck and egg trade. Their physical abnormality attracted both positive and negative attention in their home country. At one time, the King of Siam decreed that they should be put to death, having become convinced that such a conjoined birth was a "bad omen." Fortunately, the deed never took place. The Twins were 17 years old when they took advantage of an opportunity to travel the world and earn money for their mother and siblings.

They were brought to the United States in 1829 by a Captain Coffin, who had signed a contract with the young men and their mother that promised the sharing of profits from a tour in Europe and America. Unfortunately, the Captain did not keep his word, treating the Twins rather shabbily and failing to share the wealth as agreed.

When they reached the age of 21, they left Captain Coffin and toured on their own. Contrary to popular rumors, the Siamese Twins never traveled with a circus or a sideshow. Rather, they appeared in meeting halls, public buildings and museums. They were regularly seen at museums run by the eccentric naturalist, Charles Willson Peale in New York City, Philadelphia, Albany and Baltimore, where, for the admission fee, patrons could view natural wonders from the past, as well as see the Twins as a contemporary wonder of nature.

After 11 years of touring, they were tired of show business, tired of being stared at, tired of being valued only because they were "different." They began to search for a place to settle down. During their tours, they had been in northwestern North Carolina and had grown to love the area, not only because of its beauty, but also its plentiful fishing and hunting, two of their favorite pastimes. In addition, the people in the area shared their values of industry and honesty. The settlers in the area also believed in "live and let live," and Eng and Chang hoped that in that kind of environment they might be able to live like other people.

In October of 1839, Eng and Chang became naturalized citizens. Because the forms required that a surname be shown, they took the name of Bunker from a New York family who were good friends. During the same month, they bought 100 acres of land in northwestern North Carolina in Wilkes County. The property was wild and isolated and bordered a mountain creek. The records show that theirs was the first deed given in the area, and that they used a bag of silver coins to pay for the original acreage.

Those were busy times. In addition to building and furnishing a two-story house, they opened up a country store. But those were not the best economic times, so they closed the store. The two had acquired additional acreage and began farming the land. They studied the latest information on growing techniques and used those procedures. They were among the first farmers in the state to grow "bright leaf" tobacco, a variety much in demand for cigarettes.

At a local friend's wedding, Chang was smitten by Adelaide Yates, who was attending the function with her sister, Sally. In a fortunate twist of fate, Eng was favorably impressed by Sally, and soon both young men were trying to arrange to see the young women socially. Unfortunately, the girls' parents were not happy about the situation, apparently being less concerned about their physical abnormality than the fact that the men were foreign-born. But love overcame all obstacles, and the Twins married the Yates sisters in April of 1843.

The two couples moved into the large two-story house that the Twins had built with an eye to their future. In it was an extra-wide staircase, double-sized chairs and heavy furniture. The bed had been custom built to be extra wide to plan for as normal a life as possible under the circumstances.

After two years and the addition of four children, even the specially built house began to feel small. An additional 2,000 acres was secured in adjacent Surry County, a new house constructed, and the families moved to their new home, located some 3 miles from Mount Airy. This arrangement sufficed for about 10 years, but by that time, with the family members plus slaves now numbering close to 60 people, a new plan needed to be developed.

The entire acreage belonging to Eng and Chang was surveyed and divided equally. A second house was built so that Chang, Adelaide, and the members of their family would live in one house, and Eng, Sally, and their family would call the other house their home.

A schedule was agreed to whereby the Twins would alternate living in each other's house every three days. When they were in Chang's home, Eng was silent and passive, interfering in no way in Chang's affairs. The same situation prevailed when Chang was in Eng's house, as the other twin would not enter into the conversation in any way. In fact, it was said that if in the course of conversation Chang expressed the need to buy corn, and Eng had corn for sale, he would not mention it, as that would break their written agreement. This arrangement was religiously maintained until their deaths.

Although physically the closest of twins, Chang and Eng had very different personalities. The shorter of the two, Chang had the more dominant personality. Eng was quieter and more retiring, with an interest in more intellectual endeavors. Chang appeared mentally quicker, but had a short temper.

Both twins loved to play checkers and chess, but they never played against each other. If Chang was enjoying a game of checkers with a friend, Eng would sit silently, perhaps reading a book, until the game was over. The most contention came over Eng's preference for late-night games of poker, a diversion Chang wanted nothing to do with. Having to be present unto the wee hours of the morning, Chang would express his displeasure with disapproving looks and body posture, since verbal complaints were forbidden by their agreement. If Chang was invited to a friend's house for dinner, the other twin would sit silently during the evening, and as the two were leaving, Eng would say to the host, "I will pay my visit to you at some future time."

There were times when it was necessary for them to travel out of town together in order for one or the other of the twins to keep an appointment. They did have a wry sense of humor and would occasionally use their unusual situation to play a joke on others. The story is told that once they were traveling to Raleigh on the train. When the conductor came by and asked for tickets, Eng gave him his ticket promptly.

When the conductor put out his hand for the other twin's ticket, Chang remarked,with a twinkle in his eye, "I have no ticket, and I have no money." The conductor, dutifully following rules and regulations, threatened to put Chang off the train.

At that point Eng spoke up and said, "I'm afraid you can't do that, sir. I have given you my ticket, and I am entitled to ride on this train. You can't throw my brother off without me, and I refuse to move."

Confronted with an impossible situation, and with the hearty laughter of the rest of the passengers ringing in his ears, the conductor gave up his quest and made a hasty retreat into the next car. It was reported that Chang, having very much enjoyed the moment, was careful to present the conductor with his ticket later during the trip.

The Twins lived their lives as gentlemen farmers with their wives and growing families, and through the years would be blessed with 21 children between them. The families participated fully in community activities. Adelaide and Sally were very active churchgoers and the Twins gave the land on which the White Plains Baptist Church was built. A special pew was crafted for Eng and Chang so that they would be more comfortable when they attended services.

Over the years the Twins became concerned about providing for their families, especially paying for the education of the children. Unlike other families in the late 1800's, they were insistent that all the girls in the families receive a good education, just like the boys. Although Chang and Eng did not like being on display for money, they realized that it provided them with their best opportunity to support and educate their large families.

Accordingly, they decided to participate in an exhibit in New York managed by Phineas T. Barnum. Contrary to popular belief, this was the only time that the Siamese Twins ever worked for Barnum. Even though Eng and Chang rarely agreed on anything, they were united in their dislike for  the man. Barnum did not particularly care for them, either. However, because of the profit possibilities, they all agreed to this one exhibit.  It was later that Barnum joined with Bailey to form the famous circus; however, the Siamese Twins were proud that they were never involved in any circus operation.

Following the New York exhibit, the Twins toured California on their own, and increased their financial resources considerably. News of the possibility of a War Between The States reached them in California and they canceled their plans to visit Siam and returned home to North Carolina.

Eng and Chang had become ardent southerners and during the War Between The States, two sons, Christopher Wren Bunker and Stephen Decatur Bunker, each joined the Confederate Army. The Twins also lent money to help the Confederate cause. Unfortunately, the war caused considerable difficulty to many landowners in the South, and Eng and Chang Bunker were caught up in the same situation. Because of higher taxes and prices during the war, and the fact that the Confederate currency issued to them became worthless, the families suffered significant financial reverses.

And so, in the spring of 1865, Eng and Chang once again left home and toured to replenish the family coffers. In subsequent years they occasionally went on tour in the United States and also in Europe, meeting with royalty and government leaders.

From time to time the Twins would become weary with the physical restraints of their lives and seek a surgeon who would be willing to separate them. When they insisted that their local physician, Dr. Joe Hollingsworth, perform the operation, he was very direct in his rejoinder.

"Very well; just get up on that table and I'll fix you. Which would you prefer, that I should sever the flesh that connects you or cut off your heads? One will produce just about the same results as the other."

They sought opinions from prominent surgeons in both the United States and Europe, and the answer was always the same: the Siamese Twins could not be separated without risking one or both of their lives.

In 1870, Chang suffered a stroke while returning from a trip overseas, and never completely regained his health. In the following years the Twins tried to keep as normal a schedule as possible, with Eng supporting the weight of Chang's right leg and arm in a leather device fashioned by Dr. Hollingsworth.

One Monday night in January of 1874, Eng and Chang went to Chang's home to spend the customary three days. Chang came down with a severe cough and chest pains, which the doctor diagnosed as bronchitis. Eng remained in good health, unaffected by his twin's illness.

When the time came on Thursday morning for the Twins to make the two-mile trip to Eng's house, Dr. Hollingsworth advised Chang to stay home a little longer, as he was weak from the illness. Both Eng and Adelaide, Chang's wife, agreed, and begged him not to go out in the cold, raw weather. Chang would not hear of it, and insisted that their long-established living arrangements be honored. Soon, the brothers got into an open carriage and traveled in freezing weather to Eng's home.

During that day and the next, Chang continued to grow worse, experiencing severe coughing and chest pains both during the day and throughout the night. On Friday evening, because Chang could not breathe well while lying down, Eng sat up with him until they both fell asleep after midnight. At about 4 a.m., Eng's son, William, decided to check on his father and uncle. He found his father sleeping soundly, but realized that his Uncle Chang was dead.

William screamed out in alarm, waking his father suddenly. When Eng found that his twin had died, he exclaimed, "Then I am going too!" During the next hour or so, Eng cried out in panic, his body jerking frantically before falling into semi-consciousness.

As soon as Chang's death had been discovered, a boy had been dispatched on horseback to summon Dr. Hollingsworth. By the time the doctor arrived, it was too late: Eng was gone. The Siamese Twins lived to be nearly 63 years old.

Eng and Chang Bunker are buried at the White Plains Baptist Church cemetery.

⚬⚬ ⚬⚬

❖   The Siamese Twins were world famous long before 1839, when, at the age of 28, they settled in northwestern North Carolina. During their lives Mark Twain wrote essays about them, and the renowned photographer, Matthew Brady, photographed them. They were welcomed by many famous people and dignitaries including President Andrew Johnson, Queen Victoria of England, and Czar Alexander II of Russia.

When they died they left a unique legacy that went far beyond their unconventional appearance. Their reputation for honesty, hard work, and commitment to learning, would be envied by those who have had far less to overcome. Over a thousand of their descendants have continued to amplify the impact of the lives of the Siamese Twins. We would all be most fortunate to have left such a worthy heritage.

❖ ❖

❖   Eng and Chang were amazingly physically active in their younger years. They could walk six or seven miles, and swim moderate distances. Audiences were astonished as they watched the Twins perform somersaults and back-flips.

❖   One of Chang's grandsons was Caleb Vance Haynes. A highly acclaimed aviator in World Wars I and II, he was one of the famed Flying Tigers in WWII. He flew the first bomber across the Atlantic Ocean, and was the first American pilot to try to fly from the U. S. to South America over the Andes. He rose to the rank of Brigadier General and received the Silver Star and Distinguished Service Cross. Additional information on him is contained in Chapter 5, "A Big War Comes to a Small Town."

❖   One of Eng's great-great granddaughters, Tanya Rees, currently serves as the Executive Director of the Surry Arts Council and is responsible for significant planning and execution of "Mayberry Days."

❖   The Mount Airy Visitors' Center has a room devoted to the Siamese Twins with many interesting pictures and printed information.

❖   The White Plains Baptist Church, burial place of the Siamese Twins, is located on Old U.S. 601 South of Mount Airy. A state marker identifying the cemetery is in front of the church.

❖   The first home that the Siamese Twins built and brought Adelaide and Sally to as their brides, can be viewed from the intersection of U.S 601 and the 601 Bypass just south of Mount Airy.

❖   It is interesting to note the following:

During the autopsy on the Siamese Twins, the band of flesh which connected them was found to contain a continuation of the pouch lining of the abdominal cavity, an extension of liver substance from each abdomen, and some vein and liver connections.

Although very complicated surgery is now in use to separate conjoined twins, the methods and medications available at the time would not have permitted a successful separation. All the experts of the day were correct in their decision not to operate.

In spite of sharing parts of the liver, Eng, who was a teetotaler, never showed any effects when Chang drank alcoholic beverages, no matter what the quantity.

❖   Many years later an Associated Press journalist reported on a national medical conference at which  the  Siamese Twins were discussed. Dr. Worth B. Daniels, a clinical professor of medicine at Georgetown University Medical School, told the doctors of his discovery of a copy of the autopsy report that had been done after the Twins' deaths. The document stated that the physical evidence indicated a "profound disturbance of the nervous system." After studying the report in detail, Dr. Daniels came to the conclusion that Eng died of shock and fright, not because of any specific medical reason.

# 14 | *A Wish Before Dying*

EX-SHERIFF C. H. HAYNES had been feeling poorly for a few weeks and, at the urging of his family and friends, had cut back on his regular activities and was taking it easy at his home on Rockford Street.

His wife had served him breakfast on a table in the parlor, so that he could sit in his favorite chair and look out the front windows.

"Actually, hon, I'm feeling a little better this morning, ʾbut I 'preciate ya waitin' on me," he commented, between bites of buckwheat pancakes covered with sourwood honey.

About that time he spotted a long black hearse from the Moody Funeral Home coming to a stop in front of his house.

"Hey Mary, what's a hearse doin' stopping in front of our house." Didn't I tell ya I didn't feel bad enuf to go to thuh hospital? I sho' don't need no hearse cummin' afta me!"

Mrs. Haynes laughed, and answered the knock at the front door. "Well, good morning Wade, what brings you over this way today?"

"Sorry to disturb you so early, Ma'am. I need to see your husband if he's feeling up to it."

79

"Sure, come on in; he's in the parlor," Mrs. Haynes replied, ushering the visitor into the room.

"Why Wade Moody—what in tarnation are ya doin' here?" Haynes asked, his voice trembling.

"Didn't mean to upset you, Sheriff," Mr. Moody replied, " but one of your old friends, Early Collins, died over at Dobson yesterday."

The Sheriff sighed and looked away. When he spoke, there was a catch in his voice. "Waal, I'm sho sorry to hear that. Early was a good man," Haynes paused, swallowed, and then continued, "— and a good friend. He'll be missed."

The undertaker hesitated, and then continued. "Sheriff, I came over to tell you that Early's last request was to have his body prepared and placed in a coffin, with his hands folded across his breast. Then, he wanted us to call you in, and have you place his favorite brand of cigar between his fingers. Only then did he feel he would be ready to be put in the ground."

Wade Moody paused briefly, and then continued, "The last time I saw you, Sheriff, you looked a mite peak-ed. So as to make it easier on you, I decided to bring the body on over to your house and make it convenient for you to satisfy his request."

There was a long minute of silence, and then a careful reply. "That was mighty thoughtful of ya, Wade, but frankly, the thought of placing that ceegar between Early's fingers takes thuh starch outta me. I'm afraid that if I went out there, and saw dear old Early laid out, ya'd have two of us to take away for burryin'."

Sheriff Haynes sat up straight in the chair, composed himself, and with the voice of authority said, "Tell you what, I'll deputize ya to carry out Early's wish in my place."

"I'd be plumb pleased to do it for you, Sheriff," Wade replied, "and I do hope you gets to feelin' better."

"I gar-un-tee ya I'll feel a lot better once ya git that herse of yours out from in front of my house," Haynes responded, now looking more relaxed and beginning to laugh.

As the long black vehicle pulled away from the curb, Sheriff Haynes remarked to his wife, "Ya know, Early always said that he loved his ceegars better'n anything else in thuh world. Guess he really meant it!"

## TAGS *Notes:*

Episode

#107   "Gomer Pyle, U.S.M.C."
Mentions Nelson Funeral Home. In earlier days Mr. Nelson had a funeral home in Mount Airy. Later funeral operations were taken over by Moody's, and Moody's Funeral Home still exists Mount Airy.

#155   "The Arrest of the Fun Girls"
Andy promises Monroe to send him some sourwood honey. It's produced in the Mount Airy area, and many people, (including the author) think it's the BEST!

# 15 | The Music of Spring

IT WAS A BRIGHT SPRING DAY and folks were happy that winter was finally over and the weather good enough for work outdoors. Out on Route Five, Sam Jones' wife was in their yard tending to the flower garden, while their young daughter chased orange and blue butterflies.

While the two were occupied, a frequent visitor to the yard slipped unnoticed up the stairs and inside the house. The sound of music for dancing wafted down the hall, enticing the visitor to make his way into the living room. A large oval Philco radio sat on the mahogany sideboard, sending out a variety of melodious notes into the air. Unable to resist, the visitor sought out the ladder-backed chair in front of the radio and settled in to enjoy the tunes.

He was still there when Mrs. Jones came back into the house and walked into the living room.

"Oh, my goodness!" she shouted, startled at the scene in front of her.

The sharpness of her outcry did not seem to disturb the visitor at all. No indeed! In fact, by now the four-foot long black snake had wound himself around the top section of the chair and had his head pressed against the radio where the sound was loudest. Not only that, but his head was moving back and forth in time to the music coming out of the loud speaker. The announcer was entreating the audience to "Swing and Sway With Sammy Kaye" and, by golly, that's just what that big black reptile was doing.

The snake was so charmed by the strains of music that he didn't even notice the entrance, some fifteen minutes later, of a neighbor man Mrs. Jones had called in handle the unusual situation.

It was said that the demise of the sleek, black visitor was harmonious.

# 16 | *Why is Everybody Always Pickin' On Me?*

"I DON'T KNOW WHAT THE PROBLEM IS—I'm not a dangerous man," Britt Flemming said, "It just seems I run afoul of the law at odd times."

And even times too. In fact, Flemming had garnered an even fifty-six arrests by the time of his 39th birthday, a record for Surry County. In most cases he would pay his fine or serve his time. But then there were the occasions when he would manage to slip away from road work camps he had been assigned to for passing bad checks or other charges.

Being arrested, fined and thrown in jail had become an fairly steady occupation for Flemming. Many stories were told regarding his escapades.

One was that a number of years ago, when Judge H. H. Llewellyn was serving as Chief of the Mount Airy Police Department, he arrested Flemming and, after his trial and conviction, the Chief chose to personally escort the young man to Durham to serve his time in the jail there. When Chief Llewellyn returned to Mount Airy, he was walking up Main Street when he spied Flemming sauntering toward him down the street. A phone call verified that the prisoner had escaped from the jailers in Durham and had some-how made his way back home quicker than the Chief had.

On another occasion, Flemming was in a Reidsville court facing drunk and disorderly, when he put on a first-class tear-jerking scene before the local Judge.

"Your Honor," Britt pleaded, tears welling up in his eyes, "Please don't put me in jail! You know I don't have any money, Your Honor, but I don't know what I'll do if you put me in jail!" The accused dropped his head in a dramatic gesture of despair.

Suddenly, Britt raised his head up and with a pleading look on his face faced the Judge. "I know what, Your Honor," he said, holding out his right hand, "you see this ring on my finger? Now, I wouldn't sell this ring to anyone for less than $1000. But, I'll give this valuable ring off my hand right now as my bond. I know you're an honorable man, and you'll keep it safe for me."

The Judge, not having encountered Mr. Flemming previously, agreed to the deal and took the ring. When the prisoner failed to appear on the court date, the ring was sent to a local jeweler for sale to satisfy costs.

"'Fraid I can't help you this time, Jedge. Reckon it's not worth much more than a dime," the jeweler reported to a embarrassed officer of the court.

The recurring theme of passing bogus checks was the major feature that earned Flemming the record 56th arrest. Again, Flemming didn't understand why they were pickin' on him.

"I'm not guilty of forgery," he said. "All I did was sign a few fake names to bad checks."

# 17 | *All God's Creatures*

IT WAS A FRIDAY EVENING after dinner at my grandparents house. Mother had gone out to play Rook with her friends, and so I got to spend the night at the house on Church Street.

Grandmother believed that every waking minute should be productive. She reminded me frequently that "idle hands are the Devil's mischief." And so this evening, although the supper dishes had been washed, dried and put away, and all the straightening up had been finished, she would not permit herself to "do nothing."

This evening she had decided to take the opportunity to teach me how to repair the crocheted medallions on a bedspread she had made many years ago. While we worked, Grandfather enjoyed the rocking chair, as he read every word of the weekly edition of *The Mount Airy News*. In the background, hymns were softly playing on the radio.

"Well, I'll be derned. That oughta be a sight worth seeing," he remarked to nobody in particular. "Yes siree, I'm just gonna make it a point to do that! And I jest might take Miss Jewell with me. You don't have anything you have to do in the mornin', do you honey?"

"No, I don't. If it's okay with Mother, I'd love to go with you. Where're we going?"

I jumped up and ran over to the rocking chair and he immediately pulled the paper away so that I could not see what he had been reading.

"Never mind, we'll just make it a surprise."

Saturday morning I was up early and ready to go, but Grandmother made sure I ate all my scrambled eggs, ham and fried apples, before she would let me leave with my grandfather.

He drove out the highway towards Lowgap. Wherever we were going, it was way out in the country. Finally, after about 20 minutes, I saw a house and barn on the right side of the highway with ten or twelve cars parked in front of it. "Is that where we're going?"

"Sure is," he replied with a smile, bringing the Roadster to a stop. I jumped out of the car and we walked together toward the house and barn.

"Come with me, honey, I've got something special to show you." Grandfather took ahold of my hand and led me into the back of the barn area.

As we entered the enclosure, I saw a group of adults and children all gathered around a small animal lying in the straw. Grandfather brought me closer to the group.

"You may never see anything like this again in your life, Jewell. I 've never seen one before in all my years."

Several people stepped back as we approached, allowing us entry into the circle and a clear view. There in the hay was a young calf, a beautiful golden color, well fleshed out and healthy looking. The calf's four eyes were big and beseeching.

"She's got two heads!" I blurted out. The others in the group gave me a disapproving look; but I knew good and well that they must have said the same thing when they first saw the animal.

"I've talked to the County Agent, and Doc Jackson, the veterinarian, and they don't really understand what makes this happen. One of God's mysteries, I reckon. You have so much curiosity about life, Jewell, I thought you'd find this interesting." Grandfather reached down and petted one of the heads.

"Will she be alright?" I asked. She was such a pretty calf.

Grandfather shook his head and responded softly,
"'Fraid not, sugar, the Doc says they've never known one to last past a year."

Carefully sitting down in the straw, I moved close to the calf and gingerly began to pet the creature. Her skin felt like velvet. She turned one of the heads toward me and nuzzled my arm. I reached over and stroked the other head. She gave no resistance, just lay in the straw and accepted my attentions without protest. It seemed that the look in her eyes was letting me know she was glad I was there with her.

Being with this special creature was wonderful, and I would have been happy to spend the rest of the day with her. After a few minutes, Grandfather finished his conversation with the men standing around and motioned to me that it was time to leave.

Reluctantly, after placing soft kisses on both of the heads, I got up from the ground, brushing the straw off of my red gingham dress. The calf was so calm and gentle, and those big eyes were so beautiful. But there was a lot I didn't understand. And whenever I didn't understand something, I looked to Grandfather for an explanation.

"Why would God let a creature like that be born, if it can't live to grow up?" I wiped the tears from my face.

Grandfather had a soft smile on his face as he reached over and patted me gently on the head.

"Maybe it's to show us that we're supposed to love and appreciate all of God's creations, whatever they look like, and for however long they are with us. It's the least we can do."

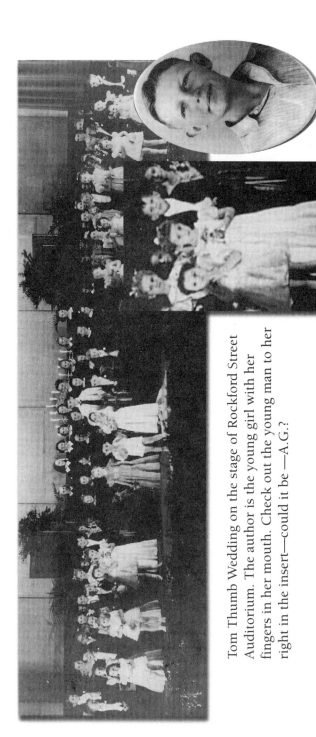

Andy as a young boy

*Photo courtesy of The Andy Griffith Museum, Mount Airy Visitors Information Center.*

Tom Thumb Wedding on the stage of Rockford Street Auditorium. The author is the young girl with her fingers in her mouth. Check out the young man to her right in the insert—could it be —A.G.?

# 18 | *Let Your Conscience Be Your Guide*

SOMETIMES IT TAKES THE PASSAGE of a good spell of time before a man begins to to listen to his conscience. For some people, it takes awhile for the inner voice to be heard in the outer world.

It was June of 1939, and George E. Welch, Mount Airy's Treasurer at the time, was at his desk preparing to open the morning mail. One letter was addressed to him personally, without his title of Treasurer, and so he decided to open that one first.

He slipped his favorite tortoiseshell letter opener into the slightly bulging envelope, being careful not to disturb its unknown contents. What he pulled out of the envelope was a real surprise: there were two $5 bills and the following note of explanation.

> "Dear Sir:
>     Several years ago your father, G.C. Welch, made a $10 mistake in cashing a check. I am restoring the money to you and you can do with it as you see fit.
>                         Conscience money,
>                                 Your friend."

As he reported this occurrence to his friends, Mr. Welch explained that his father had operated a business in Mt. Airy from 1890 until his death in 1928. However, G. C. Welch had not taken an active part in the business for five or six years prior to his passing. It appeared, therefore, that the mistake the letter writer referred to must have occurred at least twenty years ago.

As Mr. Welch's father had been a founder of the Mount Airy Friends Church, he decided to turn the cash over to the treasurer of the church, to add to their fund to help those in need.

"Waal, sir," Mr. Welch remarked, "I guess it's never too late to do the right thing!"

## TAGS *Notes:*

Episode

#144    "Goober Takes A Car Apart"
        Goober says that he thinks that Alice Nathan is a Quaker.

Mount Airy had a rich diversity of religious groups for a small town. In addition to more well-known denominations, there were good-sized congregations of both the Moravians and Friends, also known as Quakers.

SECTION FOUR

# Wisdom of a
# Country Judge

Judge Anderson Edward Creed and Mary Ellen Creed

Grandparents' home at 139 (now 134) Church Street. Many of the stories in the following two sections took place in this house.

# 19 | Do Unto Others

SUPPER WAS BARELY OVER WHEN a knock was heard on the front door. "I'll get it, Ellen," my grandfather said to my grandmother who was removing the last of the serving dishes from the dinner table.

"Might as well, Ed," she replied, "More'n likely it's for you."

Rising from his chair and brushing crumbs from his gray vest, Judge Creed strode purposefully down the hall to the front door. Not wanting to miss anything, I stuck my head around the corner, ever alert for adult conversation.

The man at the door was a good bit shorter than my grandfather, but the width of his middle section protruded past both sides of grandfather's slender waist. In the dim light, I could see that the visitor was wearing a faded pair of overalls with an equally faded blue and green plaid flannel shirt. He was holding a battered work hat in his gnarled, sun-reddened hand, which shook slightly as he spoke.

"Sorry, didn' mean to bother ya, Jedge, but frankly, I needs help and I don't know where else tuh turn."

I heard the firm, but gentle voice of my grandfather inquire, "What seems to be the problem, Cleve?"

"Well, ya know here lately my Mary's been real sickly, and I've gotta take her to a doc down in Winston-Salem. I won't get ma money for the tater crop 'til the end of thuh month and - I was a'wondering - could ya, maybe - I hate ta trouble ya and all, but —" His voice trailed off as if he couldn't bring himself to make a direct request.

"It's OK, Cleve—how much do you need?" Grandfather's voice was gentle and reassuring.

"Oh, Jedge Creed—I reckon a ten oughta do it. I'll pay ya back come Friday two weeks."

Grandfather reached into his pocket and removed a worn leather money clip. Slowly and precisely he fingered through the bills, removing the single bill requested and placed it in the man's hand.

"Cleve, I'm glad to be able to help you out. You're a good, hard-working man, and I respect the way you look after your Mary. I look forward to seeing you two weeks from Friday, and I know you will be able to pay me back then. I'm glad this will help tide you over until things turn around for you. Hope Mary gets feeling better soon."

The porch light falling on Cleve's face revealed relief, gratitude and what could very well be interpreted as a look of love.

"Oh thankya, thankya, Jedge. Miss Mary an' I sho' do 'preciate ya help. You'll see. I'll be back here Friday two weeks ta pay you back—and I'll bring a mess of taters for ya and the missus, too. Thankya, Thankya!"

As the man turned and walked down the porch stairs, Grandfather closed the door, a gentle smile of satisfaction on his face. When he returned to the dining room, he walked over to our maid and cook, who had just finished cleaning off the dining room table and sweeping up any crumbs that had fallen to the floor.

"Mighty tasty greens tonight, Lillian. Mizz Ellen's cornbread was special good dunked in that de-licious pot likker."

"Glad ye liked 'em, Jedge. I sho enjoyed makin' 'em fer ya." Lillian picked up the broom and walked back through the swinging door into the kitchen, her face beaming at the compliment.

Grandmother reset the fruit centerpiece on the table, placing it carefully in the center of the doily she had herself crocheted. Straightening herself up to her full five feet, she faced Grandfather squarely.

"It was another one of them, wasn't it? Ed, that was the fourth one this week!" Shaking her head so that the bun of dark brown hair on the back moved to and fro, she continued, "Ed, you're going to give us into the poorhouse!"

"Now, Ellen," he gently retorted, "They're good people. They just need someone to have faith in them and give them a helping hand now and then."

My grandmother gave him 'the look' and continued straightening up the rest of the room.

It was a familiar exchange. I had heard my grandfather say, "Now, Ellen," and my grandmother refer to the "poorhouse" so often that I felt I should ask someone just where that particular house was.

Grandfather smiled and motioned for me to come to his side. He reached down, put his hand on my shoulder and said, "You know, honey, I've always found that giving to others is good for my soul."

"Time for you to start gettin' ready for bed, Jewell," Grandmother reminded me, and I reluctantly started to make my way up the stairs. As my feet reached the first landing, I heard her say to Grandfather, "Oh, by the way Ed, I left the back porch light on. Lillian's brother came by earlier to see you about something. I reckon he'll be back soon." And with the final phrase, I heard the sigh that indicated an upward roll of her eyes.

This tender routine was replayed week after week: the light-skinned folks came to the front door, and the dark-skinned folks to the back porch. Regardless of the location, Grandfather's demeanor and response to people was the same. Although he did not give to everyone, only a small number heard him say, "Sorry, I don't think you're ready to take on the responsibility of a loan just yet."

In spite of my grandmother's concerns, I witnessed the repayment of a great many of the loans. Grandfather's approach was simple: first, affirm the person's capabilities; second, set clear expectations and timing for repayment; and above all, respect the dignity of the individual.

It was no surprise to me that my grandfather, Judge A. E. Creed, enjoyed the esteem and affection of so many people in the community.

# 20 | *What It Was— Was Baseball*

THE CRACK OF THE BAT on the baseball reverberated throughout the stands, and the capacity crowd cheered the first hit of the game. I screamed and jumped up and down. It was wonderful to actually be in the stands watching a baseball game.

Reddick Field, behind Mount Airy High School, was the scene of all the sporting events in town. One side of the high fence bordered my grandparents' property, and whenever there was a game, I would bring a blanket and sit on the ground, my face pressed against a hole in the boards to catch all the action.

I especially liked the baseball games. Grandmother rented the downstairs bedrooms to baseball players on the State Circuit when they were in town. It was exciting to talk with them- they had been so many places and had so many interesting stories to tell. Mother was concerned about my hanging around them, but Grandmother and Grandfather assured her that it was good for me to be exposed to people who had lived in bigger towns than Mount Airy.

Earlier this week, my Grandfather told me he had bought tickets for the two of us to go to what he described as a special event on Saturday afternoon.

"You'll get a kick out of this, Jewell," he said, with a mischievous smile and a wink at Grandmother. "We'll be right there for all the action."

When Saturday afternoon finally arrived,we entered the grandstand and Grandfather gave our tickets to a man wearing the uniform of The American Legion, the sponsors of the event. On the way to our seats, Grandfather stopped one of the vendors to stock up on refreshments. He bought his favorite, Dr. Pepper, got me a bottle of Orange Crush, and balancing a large box of popcorn between us, we made our way down the stairs to our seats. We stopped at almost every row as Grandfather responded to men and women calling out greetings. All this took so long that I was afraid that the game would start before we got to our places.

Our seats were right behind home plate with a great view of the whole field. Grandfather believed in getting the best seats you could afford at any event. I gave him a hug and a kiss. "Thank you Grandfather for bring me to the baseball game. I love baseball."

He mentioned something about this being a special kind of baseball game. I didn't really care what kind of game it was. I was spending the afternoon with my grandfather, and sitting in these seats was sure better than peeking through a knothole.

I found out soon what Grandfather meant by "a special kind of game." Few people in the crowd had ever seen a baseball game quite like this one. I surely hadn't. They had a pitcher, catcher, batters and players on the bases and in the field. The difference was that each man was sitting on a donkey, and all plays required the players to convince the donkeys to move in the direction needed to complete the play. Most of the time the donkeys were totally uninterested in assisting in the process. It was *so* funny!

When the batter hit the ball into left field, he had to convince his donkey to trot over to first base before the ball was thrown back to the first baseman. Generally, he had plenty of time to do that however, as the poor fellow in left field had a terrible time getting his animal to go anywhere near the area where the ball had landed, so that he had to get down off his donkey, pick up the ball, get back on the donkey and then throw the ball to the first baseman. The umpires were on donkeys also which precluded any close-up inspection of most of the plays.

As best I remember, it took five to ten minutes to complete the first play and the crowd was laughing so hard, it was impossible to hear what anybody was saying on the field. I laughed so hard I wet my pants, but looking at the grown-ups around me, they looked as if they had wet their pants also.

Thankfully, the game was over in less than the normal nine innings. Neither players nor spectators would have lasted that long.

Grandfather took me to see Donkey Baseball every year until I was in my teens. It was one of our favorite things to do together.

**Andy to Helen:**
"I trust you because you don't lie to me."

**Helen to Andy:**
"Then why do you lie to me?"

**Andy to Helen:**
"I lie to you because you don't trust me!"

—*Episode #226: "Andy's Trip To Raleigh"*

# 21 | Eyes and Lies

BETTER HURRY, JEWELL. *Get the story straight in your mind,* the voice in my head cautioned.

"It'll be okay, I'm not gonna worry." I spoke out loud to silence my fears. It was after 5 o'clock and I was just now going home. My grandmother would have lots of questions, for sure. When I left for school this morning, I had no idea what would happen during the day.

When I arrived at school this morning, our regular fourth grade teacher, Miss Dora Valentine, was out sick. The Principal had assigned a substitute, Miss Allred, who was just out of college, new in town, and not familiar with the normal rules and regulations. At the noon recess, Mary Nell, Sylvia and I had laughed about Miss Allred's bumbling attempts to keep order, and how the Midkiff twins, Ronald and Donald, had conned her into not taking up the previous day's homework.

I'm not sure which one of us was the first to suggest that we skip school for the afternoon. None of us had never done anything like that before, and I was sure we'd get caught. But Mary Nell agreed with Sylvia that if we were ever gonna get by with playing hooky, today was the day!

Back in the room after the lunch break, the three of us tried to act normal, although I was sure my face betrayed the guilt I was already feeling. Suddenly, Sylvia gave out a loud moan and clutched her hands over her stomach. Startled, Miss Allred jumped up and ran to Sylvia's desk.

"Ooo - ooh, mm- mm, aa-ah." Sylvia's groans became louder. Mary Nell and I displayed the looks of surprise and great concern that we had carefully practiced during recess.

"What's the matter, honey?" Miss Allred asked uneasily.

"It's - it's my sto-mach, pa-ins in my sto-mach!" Sylvia's cries were so real that for a minute she had me worried. *She should have tried out for the class play. She really knows how to lay it on.*

"Come on, honey," Miss Allred took Sylvia's hand. "I'll take you down to the nurse's office." As she started to leave, she noticed the Midkiff twins smiling and winking at the other boys seated by the window. The teacher hesitated for a minute, giving Mary Nell the opportunity she was looking for.

"It's all right, teacher, I'll go with her." Mary Nell moved quickly from her desk to Sylvia's side.

"And I'll help her," I shouted. "We're all friends."

*Oh, why did you tell her you were friends?* The voice in my head scolded me. *She'll be suspicious for sure now!*

"That's very nice of you girls, but I don't think we need both you to go with her to the nurse." Miss Allred put her arms around Sylvia's waist and began to help her up from her seat.

"Ooo-oo-ooh, aa-aaah." Sylvia clasped her stomach and leaned over as if she were going to fall to the floor.

Just then, Dean Bray shot me a knowing look and a wink and motioned to several of the other students to follow him to the pencil sharpener. Ordinarily, I'd been happy to have that much attention from Dean, but all I could think of was that if he knew Sylvia was faking, surely Miss Allred would figure it out soon.

The line at the pencil sharpener was getting longer and the resulting conversation and shuffling of feet increasingly louder.

"Well, all right." Miss Allred motioned to Mary Nell and me. "You girls help her down to the nurse's office right away, ya hear?"

She shot a look at the group at the pencil sharpener. "Maybe I'd better stay here with the class."

Mary Nell and I sounded like yodelers as our words tumbled over one another. "We'll take care of her!"

Miss Allred gave us a strange look, but didn't stop us. Several paper airplanes were now flying across the room, along with a couple of spitballs, diverting her attention. Thank goodness for the Midkiff twins!

Just in case Miss Allred might be watching, Sylvia was careful to keep up the moaning and groaning as we held her by each arm and helped her as she struggled to walk to the end of the hall and down the stairs toward the nurse's office.

As soon as we were out of sight, we ducked under the stairs and picked up our satchels where we had left them at recess. Quickly, Mary Nell and I followed Sylvia as she led us out the side entrance onto the playground.

"Go to the back of the playground where the trees are," she whispered. "Nobody can see us from the windows if we walk in the woods.

We walked behind a couple of houses, took a short cut over to the middle of the Spring Street hill, and headed down the hill to Sylvia's house. Her mother worked at Efrid's Department Store and wouldn't be home, so we'd have the house all to ourselves. Sylvia snuck us in the back door and hoped the neighbors wouldn't notice.

We ate Moon Pies and drank RC Cola until we all felt a little sick. Sylvia had a super collection of paper dolls, and we threw ourselves into their imaginary worlds and tried to forget Rockford Grammar School and Miss Allred. But I couldn't forget. My stomach was tied up in knots. Sylvia would shush me when I wondered if anybody had missed us, but I could tell that Mary Nell was also beginning to worry.

Sylvia had no such concerns. She was focused on making the most of the adventure. "Let's go to your house, Mary Nell. Your mother is still in Roanoke with her sister and the new baby, isn't she?"

"Well – yeah – I guess we could." Mary Nell's response was less than enthusiastic, but we all headed toward her house on Church Street determined to enjoy ourselves.

When we got to Mary Nell's we dropped our things in the kitchen and went out into the big backyard. There was a large weeping willow tree, beautiful pink and white crepe myrtles and a little pond with water lilies. Mary Nell was an only child and her father gave her anything she asked for. She had swings, see-saws, a climbing tower and a merry-go-round. The three of us took turns pushing each other on the swings, played hide and seek, and spun ourselves dizzy on the merry-go-round. After a while, I was having so much fun playing outside with my best friends on a sunny April day that I forgot everything else.

The chimes from the Presbyterian Church brought me back to reality. My goodness, it was 5 o'clock! I should have been home two hours ago. I said my goodbyes quickly, grabbed the satchel with my books in it and started hastily walking the block and a-half towards home.

My mother would be off work and at Grandmother's house by now. What in the world would I tell them? Words were tumbling in my mind as I tried to put together a story I hoped they would accept.

I found Grandmother and Mother in the dining room setting the table for supper.

"Where in the world have you been, chile? Don't you know what time it is?" Grandmother provided the questions and Mother provided the disapproving looks.

The less-than-well-crafted story poured out of my mouth. "Sylvia was real sick and the teacher asked Mary Nell and me to take her to the nurse, and the nurse said she should go home, but her mother was at work, so we took her home and stayed with her, and I'm sorry I'm so late, but I didn't want to leave Sylvia because she was so sick."

"Why didn't the nurse call Sylvia's mother at work to come take her home?" Grandmother's question was reinforced by Mother's scowl.

I hadn't thought about that question, but quickly made up a response. "Oh, the nurse did call for her mother but she had left work . . . to go to a customer's house . . . to take some measurements for a dress the lady needed altered . . . and the woman at Efrid's said she was sure it would be all right for us to take Sylvia home . . . and she'd tell Sylvia's mother as soon as she got back."

Mother took a deep breath, deepened the scowl on her face, and spoke in her most commanding tone of voice.

"Don't you ever leave school again like that, Jewell - ya hear me?"

"Yes, Ma'am. I'm sorry."

Grandmother added her bit to the discussion. "Jewell, it's fine to want to help your friends, but some things should be handled by adults. If the nurse told you to take Sylvia home, that was a poor choice on her part."

"Well, I wondered about it, but I thought she knew best." *Where did that lie come from? Gracious, it rolled out of my mouth so quickly.* I realized I'd better get out of there before I had to make up anything else.

"Do y'all need me to help you, or can I start my homework?"

"You go do your homework now. I'll call ya if I need ya," Grandmother replied.

I gave Grandmother a quick hug and left the room before Mother could say anything else.

By the time my grandfather drove up in his Model A Ford, I was sitting in the swing on the front porch carefully reading, "The History of North Carolina."

"Howdy, Jewell. See you're getting your homework done." he commented with a nod and a smile as he came up the stairs onto the porch.

"Yes, sir," I replied quickly. "This chapter is about the Lost Colony." I jumped down from the swing and opened the screen door for him.

"Do you need me to hep you bring anythin' in?" I wanted to make sure I was pleasant and cooperative with everybody this afternoon.

"No thank ya, sugar. Just keep on doin' ya homework."

After Grandfather went in the house, I tried to keep reading the history book, but my mind flopped around like a drunken chicken.

*Please God, don't let Mother and Grandmother ask me any more questions. I promise you I'll never do anything like this again.*

After a few minutes, Grandfather came back out on the porch. "Got room for me on the swing, Jewell?"

"Sure. Let me just get this book out of the way."

He took his place on the swing and turned to me. "Understand you were late in getting home today. What happened?"

*Oh no! Why did they have to say anything to him?*

My stomach started churning again and my throat was dry. I took a deep breath and repeated "the story."

Grandfather listened to my recitation. When I had finished, he reached over, took my hand and said quietly, "Jewell, I don't think I quite understand. Look at me, honey. Tell me again why you were so late getting home today."

I turned my head toward him and looked into his clear blue eyes.

"Well. . . like I said. . . Sylvia was . . . ." my voice broke into a sob and my head dropped to my chest.

Grandfather reached over and pulled my head onto his vest as he reached for his handkerchief.

"It's all right. Go ahead and cry, honey. You need to cry out the lie."

I cried and cried, wiping my eyes with his handkerchief while he patted my head. I sobbed until I could hardly catch my breath. When my cries finally dissolved into a whimper, he raised my head up and pushed the dampened hair back from my face.

"Now tell me what really happened, Jewell. Tell me all of it."

I went over the day's events, repeating the conversation on the playground at recess. When I tried to emphasize that it was Sylvia and Mary Nell's fault, that skipping school was their idea, Grandfather would have none of it.

"Shame on you, Jewell! You know better than that. Those friends of yours are only responsible for a bad idea. You are responsible for choosing to act on the bad idea, and then lying about it to boot." His voice was quiet and strong.

At every turn in my story, he would call my hand if he felt I was not owning up to my part in the escapade. His questions and my expected answers were like the Responsive Readings from the Methodist Hymnal.

"And what's the truth about that, Jewell?"

"I was wrong to do it."

"And what do you promise, Jewell?"

"It wasn't right. I won't ever do it again."

"And what happens when you lie, Jewell?"

"It hurts me as much as anybody else."

It was the longest fifteen minutes of my life, but when the cleansing ritual was finished, my stomach was quiet, I was breathing freely again, and the tears had ceased.

Grandfather stood up and lifted me down from the swing, a soft smile on his face.

"Why don't we go in the house and git washed up for supper. He put his hand on my shoulder and gave me a little squeeze.

"It's all over now, sugar. Let's eat!"

## TAGS *Notes:*

Episode

#64    "Opie's Rival"
       Opie tells several serious lies to keep Andy from going out with Peggy, the nurse. Andy's understanding, but firm approach handles the situation.

Again-
IT'S SCHOOL TIME

School books of all kinds, pencils, erasers, tablets and what not to buy—and the total amount is a considerable sum. But if you come here to buy, the cost will be much less, for we have all school supplies marked very, very close.

**Creed's Book Store**

HAS SOLD SCHOOL BOOKS TO YOU AND YOUR PARENTS

# Fire Sale By
## Creed Book Store

Insurance adjusters have completed making a settlement of the loss sustained by Creed's Book Store in the fire which so seriously damaged the stock some weeks ago, and Mr. Creed is now conducting an auction sale of the damaged goods. The sales are being held three times a day, at 10 a. m. and 2 and 8 p. m. In the lot is a quantity of sporting goods, office supplies, books and toilet articles. The sales are being held in the W. H. Marion store next to the book store.

Carpenters are now remodeling the store room of Mr. Creed, one of the changes to be made will be raising the floor on a level with the street. thus eliminating the step down into the store.

# 22 | *Milkshakes and Memories*

"JEW-ELL, TIME FOR BE-EDD," my mother singsonged from the stairs.

"Can't I stay up a little longer?" I pleaded. Grandfather said I could help him make his milkshake."

"I'll make sure she gets to bed directly, Mabel. She won't be long," Grandfather replied, winking at me. We were known for stretching our time together.

"All right, but remember, she's got school in the morning."

In the kitchen, Grandfather handed me the small metal grater and a dark brown nutmeg. "I'll need about a teaspoon-full," he said, "and be careful of your fingers." Cautiously I scraped the nutmeg against the rough edges of the grater, delighted to be entrusted with a vital part of the special recipe.

Grandfather went over to the Hamilton-Beach mixer and re-moved the tall silver-toned cup. I had often wondered just how many milkshakes this wonderful machine had prepared. It had been a fixture of the soda fountain in the Creed Book Store for many years.

My grandfather had come back to Mount Airy from Roanoke, Virginia a number of years ago to take over the bookstore business after his brother, Will, had died. In those days, all the high school students had to buy their books, and the State of North Carolina had designated our family bookstore for the purchases in this area. The store also carried cigarettes, cigars, stationery, and additional sundry items for the grown-ups. But it was the wonderful milkshakes, sundaes, and other such goodies that kept the place crowded with young people.

The Creed Book Store was no longer in operation, but the mixer, more than a foot tall, with a heavy white ceramic base, still was. Only now it was operating from a place of honor in our kitchen, faithfully churning out Grandfather's daily concoction.

When the milkman from Surry Dairy delivered four glass bottles to the front door every other morning, Grandmother knew exactly how to handle them before putting them in the Kelvinator refrigerator. Each had a two-inch layer of cream positioned in the neck of the bottle. One bottle she would turn side to side and then rotate completely, to make sure all the cream was mixed in. She would skim half the cream off the two other bottles, saving it in another container for whipped cream or other delights. The last bottle she placed in the refrigerator on the top shelf on the right side. It was set aside for Grandfather and when the time came for it to be used in his special milkshake, then, and only then, would he, and only he, decide how much cream would go into the mixture.

This night he removed the bottle and, with reckless abandon, poured *all* the cream into the milkshake container and followed it with half of the bottle of milk, leaving the remainder of milk to fend for itself. Then he took an egg from the carton, tapped it on the side of the counter and, with one smooth move, deftly opened the shell and deposited the raw egg into the milk. Next came the sugar, scooped from the green hobnail glass jar with no apparent measurement. A dash of vanilla from a bottle in the cupboard followed.

"Go ahead, Jewell, put the nutmeg in." he said, and with the flourish of an honored chef, I sprinkled the aromatic shavings on the top of the mixture.

Soon the metal cup was positioned on the stand engaging the motor and initiating the whirring of the stirrer as it did it's magic on the mix.

"Got your glass, Jewell? It won't take long." Grandfather said, unable to disguise his excitement. Although making his milkshake was a regular routine, he always acted as if it was a once-in-a-lifetime treat.

Grandfather removed the milkshake cup and began to pour a small serving into my glass. Momentarily, the thought of raw egg caused me to feel queasy, but the joy of sharing my grandfather's pleasure overcame any other ideas.

As both of us sipped and smiled, Grandfather said, "Don't forget, Jewell, a milkshake a day keeps the doctor away."

The phrase sounded somewhat familiar - but I wasn't sure. But then, nothing really mattered but sipping and sharing with my grandfather.

## TAGS *Notes:*

Episode

#131    "Barney's Physical"
        Thelma Lou gives Barney a milkshake made with raw eggs
        to help him gain weight

#213    "Helen the Authoress"
        Howard has his malted milkshakes made with raw eggs.

# Shooting Affray At "Black Cat" Friday

## Bryan McMillian Accidentally Shot In Brawl; Now Recovering.

Bryan McMillian, 23 year old Virginia youth, shot in a brawl at the Black Cat Filling Station near here late Friday night, is reported to be recovering at the Martin Memorial Hospital, where he was taken after the affair.

Hoke Smith, operator of the filling station, stated to officers that he struck a companion of McMillian's, Hermit Smith, over the head with a pistol. The gun fired, he said, and the bullet grazed Hermit Smith's chest and passed completely through McMillian's body.

Hermit Smith is reported to have been drunk, and to have been in a fight with a man named Williams earlier in the evening. He and McMillian were ordered away from the station by the proprietor, but later returned, the fight in which McMillian was shot occurring about midnight.

An investigation of the affair by Sheriff John D. Thompson seemed to bear out Smith's statement, as the trigger guard of the pistol used by Smith was bent by a blow of some sort. One cartridge in the gun had been fired. The wounded youth also corroborated the statement of the proprietor in a statement to his father this week.

Hermit Smith had a pistol with him at the time of the accident, and is said to have been brandishing it during the evening.

Hoke Smith has been placed under a bond of $300 pending the outcome of the injuries of McMillian

# 23 | *Shinin' a Light on Moonshine*

*"But I done my time, And I ain't been moonshinin'*
*since . . . well, I mean, not so as you could notice."*
—Rafe Hollister

MY GRANDFATHER ALWAYS TOLD ME, "Jewell, we've got three main industries in Mount Airy: furniture factories, knitting mills, and bootlegging—and I'm sorry to say, bootlegging's the most popular."

For most of the years when Andy Griffith and I were growing up in Surry County, it was a dry county, not allowing any production or sale of alcoholic beverages. But liquor seemed to flow freely anyway. Mount Airy was only eight miles from the Virginia border, and with alcohol sales freely permitted in the adjacent Virginia counties, there was always someone ready to bring the forbidden fruit across the border into our area. The bottles would sometimes be secreted in the farmer's boots, thus the term "bootlegging."

One time my Aunt Bea and Uncle Bill were visiting from Columbus, Georgia, and had gotten rooms at the Blue Ridge Hotel on Main Street. Noting that Uncle Bill was dressed more "nattily" that most locals and had the air of a "big city" man, the bellman approached him smiling and speaking in a conspiratorial whisper.

"Ya want me to git ya some hooch? I can git ya good stuff at a good price!"

Uncle Bill declined the offer. Aunt Bea had filled him in about the "small town" atmosphere, so he had planned ahead, bringing with him whatever supplies of that type he felt might be desirable.

There were many illegal homemade distilling operations back in the hills, where sugar, yeast and water were cooked over a fire to make wood grain alcohol. Since the work was done mainly under cover of darkness, with only the moon for illumination, the product came to be known as "moonshine."

There was one incident I remember that occurred when I was a young girl. Federal revenue agents were involved in a big raid at "The Grill" on the Fancy Gap Highway, seizing a significant amount of illegal liquor. I was very excited when the Sheriff came to the house to ask my grandfather to preside over the hearing for the two men that had just been arrested. In addition to being a Justice of the Peace, my grandfather had also been designated as U.S. Commissioner for the area. Selling non-tax-paid liquor was considered an "offense against Uncle Sam," and therefore, in these kind of cases, he was in charge of setting bonds and remanding suspects to the Federal Court at Winston-Salem.

There were other benefits of Grandfather's position. After the stills were raided and the operations dismantled, the officers would bring us blocks of camphor they had recovered. The camphor was much prized by Grandmother. She put the milky-white blocks on the shelf in the glass-front cabinet that held her heirloom silver service and silver side dishes. Incredibly, the action of the camphor kept the silver sparkling year round, without any further effort on her part.

It was difficult to deter those intent on supplying the consistent demand for alcohol products. Virtually every week *The Mount Airy News* recorded stories of stills being raided and bootleggers being fined. Owners of filling stations were prominent among those charged, apparently believing that their operating licenses enabled them to fill up both automobiles and people with high-powered fuel.

Recorder's Court Judge H. H. Llewellyn was noted for his crusade against illegal alcohol sales, giving out fines of $1000 in the 1930s, plus road work sentences. At one juncture, the Judge was so upset with what he perceived to be lax enforcement of the law, that he scolded local law enforcement officers in open court saying, "The officers should be ashamed of themselves, and do their duties better, or hand in their badges." He went so far as to call into question all cases that had been handled in Superior Court. In those where the prosecutor had elected to drop prosecution of the case, the Judge ordered them to be returned to his court for action.

In addition to illegal liquor production and sales cases, local judges presided over many charges of drunkenness. Unlike Otis on *The Andy Griffith Show*, the violators did not just walk into the jail cell and sleep it off. Fines up to $75 each with road work were assessed, and one unlucky man who was convicted of being drunk *and* cursing got to work it off during three months with a road gang.

But the situation was not without its lighter side. In early 1941, when rationing of sugar was in effect, a columnist for the *Greensboro Daily News* wrote a tongue-in-cheek column about the decline in the quality of the "mountain dew" that was now being turned out by traditional moonshiners. He questioned the caliber of the spirits when Karo syrup was being used instead of sugar, and when lemon was being left out to reduce sugar requirements. Writing in his column, and focusing on the Mount Airy area, he said, "We are just laughing up our sleeves at the bootleggers for having to put molasses instead of sugar into their brew. But, maybe now they'll leave out some of the lye and barbed wire."

Today, in spite of the fact that alcohol products can be purchased legally in many places in Mount Airy and surrounding Surry County, there are still those making "shine" in the mountains. Some of the locals still swear, "ya ain't really had a good drink 'til you've tasted our local juice."

## TAGS *Notes*

Episode

#17     "Alcohol and Old Lace"
        There are stills aplenty mentioned in this episode. Andy and
        Barney think that a still may be in operation in Fancy Gap.

(A dozen or more operators of illegal alcohol production are mentioned in various episodes of TAGS throughout the years.)

#44    "Sheriff Barney"
Barney tries to find out where Rafe Hollister's still is by probing Otis' subconscious mind.

#98    "The Haunted House"
Big Jack Anderson is running a still in the basement of an abandoned house.

#188   "The Battle of Mayberry"
Moonshine has a long history in this area. In a historical report on the Battle of Mayberry it is said that peace was made between the native Indians and the settlers when one of the settlers presented the natives with a jug of local corn liquor. (And a good time was had by all!)

❖    The slang term "hooch" is derived from "hoochinoo," a crude alcoholic liquor made by the Alaskan Indians.

# 24 | *Attacking a Gentle Heart*

THEY TOLD ME THAT MY GRANDFATHER was sick. "He's got a bad heart." How could that be? I didn't know anybody with a better, more loving heart than my grandfather.

For a couple of months now he had not seemed himself. Up until a few weeks ago, he would sit with me on the green front porch swing every afternoon and we would talk about what had happened during the day. It had been some time since he had been able to walk with me the two blocks down to "The Little Store" on Spring Street for my favorite treat, tiny wax bottles with sweet colored liquid in them. I loved to have him go with me to the store. He took great pleasure in buying extra goodies, some times even chocolate-covered cherries, as well as some licorice twists to satisfy his sweet tooth. If he was tempted to increase the variety of delicious sweets, he would stop himself, shake his head and say, "Best not take too much home at one time or your Grandmother will fuss at both of us."

Mr. Johnson, the proprietor of the store, a thin, wiry man who looked as if he had never eaten a piece of candy in his life, would put the treats in a small white waxed-paper bag, carefully folding down the top for carrying home. But we seldom ever got back to the house with the bag's contents intact. "Candy's meant to be eaten," Grandfather would say. "I reckon it won't hurt to have a piece or two on the way home."

I had been surprised when I went with him to his office a several weeks ago. Usually he would stride purposefully up the narrow wooden stairs, declaring that it was good exercise for both of us. But that day he asked me to hold his hand as we slowly climbed the worn wooden steps. I held tightly to his hand and he muttered something about being "a mite tired today."

Two weeks ago, he had taken ill and Dr. Mitchell had ordered bed rest until he felt stronger. Since climbing stairs was not permitted, Grandfather had moved into the downstairs front bedroom, prompting adjustments to the whole household's daily activities. To help out Grandmother, Mother and I had left our apartment and had taken up residence in the back bedroom on the first floor of their home.

Last week, as I was putting my school books down in the hall, I heard the worried voices of my mother and grandmother coming from the dining room.

"Now, Mother, Papa will be OK. You know he's got a lot of gumption. He's not going to let a little heart attack put him out of commission for long!"

Through the half-opened door, I could see my Grandmother, tears softly flowing down her face. It was a strange sight. My mother had always been very emotional and prone to crying, and many times I had seen Grandmother comfort and encourage her. But this time, it was Mother who was stroking Grandmother's arm and murmuring reassuring words. But as I peeked through the cracked door, I could see a look of concern on my mother's face that belied her words. I felt my stomach tie up in knots. Grandfather's spell of sickness must be serious.

Whenever possible, I would go in to see him, climbing up on the chintz-covered day bed to be close to him. When Grandmother would come in to shoo me out, he would declare, "Having Jewell around makes me feel better, Ellen. Let the chile stay."

I wanted to be near him as much as possible. A tall, sinewy, colored man named Carl, one of Lillian's cousins, had been hired to help as an orderly. Carl watched over him at night, sleeping on a cot in the room and kept close during the day to help him get out of bed, bathe, and walk around when he felt strong enough.

Lillian stayed busy in the kitchen preparing special foods for Grandfather. "Judge Creed wants some stirred custard - the doctor said it would be good for him," I heard my grandmother tell Lillian. Stirred custard had always been one of my grandfather's favorite desserts. Surely, having some now would make him feel better.

Seeing me at the kitchen door, my face betraying my concern, Lillian called out to me, "Come on in honey-chile, you can hep me." Pulling out the double boiler pans, she gave me the larger one to fill with water and place on the stove. After putting eggs, milk, sugar, vanilla and nutmeg in the top pan, she gave me my instructions. "Pull over the kitchen stool, honey, and stand on it so's you can reach the pans on the stove. I'll let you stir the custard while it's cookin'."

Proudly I accepted responsibility for this important job. I kept the wooden spoon moving gently, but consistently, in the mixture, making sure that the custard did not stick to the bottom of the pan.

"No lumps now, honey—it needs to be easy for your grandfather to swallow," Lillian warned softly.

My worry about Grandfather's condition lessened as I stirred. I was making something that would help him get well. I gave my full attention to the sacred task. When the mixture was fully cooked and cooled to a lukewarm temperature, Lillian poured the custard into Grandfather's favorite green and white bowl and set it on a lacquered tray for me to take in to him. Carl had helped Grandfather sit up in bed, tying a napkin around his neck over his nightshirt.

As Carl started to feed him, Grandfather announced, "That's OK, Carl, I'm feeling pretty strong right now. I can handle it myself. You can go now—if I need it, I'm sure Jewell will help me." I nodded vigorously in assent. As he tasted his first spoonfuls, he said, "Hot Diggity—that's really good. Did you hep make this, Jewell?"

"Yes, I did! I stirred and stirred and kept it smooth!"

"Well you did a mighty good job, honey. I swan if this isn't about the best stirred custard I've ever eaten!"

When he finished, he handed the bowl to me to return to the kitchen. "Get Carl for me, will you Jewell? I think I want to go sleep now. By the way, tell your mother and grandmother that you can sleep in here on the day bed tonight, if you want to!"

Did I want to? Of course I did. I was always hoping for the nights when he felt well enough for me to sleep in the same room. Mother and Grandmother usually turned down my pleadings—but this time he had asked for me himself!

Later in the evening, after my bath, I put on my pink and white flannel nightgown and went downstairs. There was no begging to stay up longer to listen to Edgar Bergen and Charlie McCarthy, no asking for chocolate milk and gingerbread. I said my prayers, with a special plea for Grandfather, told Mother and Grandmother good night and went into his room. If I was close by—maybe I could save his heart from harm.

During the night, I awoke to hear him snoring softly. He was better! I just knew he would be. He was better because of my stirred custard!

---

| *The Mount Airy News* | March 8, 1944 |
|---|---|

### Magistrate A. E. Creed Dies of Heart Attack

Magistrate and United States Commissioner, Anderson Edward Creed, 73, died at his home on Church Street Wednesday about 4 a.m. after an illness of several weeks of a heart ailment. He attended to business as long as he was able. His judgments were adjudged fair and impartial by his fellowmen.

The deceased was a native of Surry County and highly respected by those who knew him. He was the eldest son of Anderson and Martha Durham Creed and spent much of his life in this city, returning here from Roanoke, Va. years ago to take charge of the Creed Book Store after the death of his brother, the late Will Creed.

The body of Mr. Creed remained at the Moody Funeral Home until 9 a.m. Thursday, when it was taken back to his home on Church Street, where the funeral was held at 4 p.m. Thursday afternoon, with his pastor, the Rev. C. N. Clark, of Central Methodist Church officiating, and interment made in Oakdale Cemetary.

# My Mount Airy Kinfolk

My Aunt Bea

My Mother In Her
Flapper Days

# 25 | *Rising In Love*

MY NOSE REGISTERED THE FIRST ALERT, picking up the unmistakable smell of yeast rising from hot, still-baking dinner rolls. Dropping my third-grade school books in the parlor, I headed straight for the kitchen, only to find Lillian, our cook, just about to put the last batch in the oven. A big sigh announced my disappointment. I had missed my part. It was my job to beat the dough down after it had risen up almost over the edge of the brown and blue striped crockery mixing bowl. The bowl might as well have been fine china from the care taken with it, in spite of a couple of thumb-sized chips on the rim. Perhaps it was the fact that it housed the beginning of a miracle: light, flavorful rolls, without which the evening meal would have been incomplete. The love that infused the baking process gave this particular bowl semi-divine properties.

Lillian spoke to me in her deep, sweet voice, "Chile, you're late. Had to get the rolls movin'—couldn't wait on ya." I apologized with a hug, pressing my pigtailed head deep into her ample dark bosom.

"I'm sorry, I was jumping rope with Sylvia and plumb forgot the time." I explained, receiving a generous dusting of flour from the printed apron hanging around her neck. It was a brand new apron, even though the last one had only been worn for a couple of months. Grandmother had bought the apron, one of many fine-looking specimens. She would have preferred to buy Lillian new dresses, but that just wasn't done, and even if she had, Lillian would have been too proud to accept them. So Grandmother did her part to enhance Lillian's meager wardrobe with bright, wonderfully decorated aprons.

However, once used a short time, Grandmother would decide that each apron was no longer suitable, and replace it, giving the old ones to Lillian for "rags." If Lillian's grandchildren were ever seen wearing dresses made of similar material, no mention was ever made of it. Both Grandmother and Lillian would keep their dignity.

Since Grandmother valued industriousness, I was glad to be found wiping off the counters and putting things away when she came through the green swinging door that led to the kitchen from the hall.

"How's it comin' along, Lillian?" she inquired, glancing around the room.

"Right fine, Mizz Ellen," Lillian replied. (This more familiar name was employed with family, but it would have been "Mizz Creed" had any outsiders been present.)

"Jewell," Grandmother continued, "make sure you pay 'tention to what Lillian shows you. You'll have to know how to do this when you cook for a family of yer own some day."

I often thought it curious that my mother, her daughter, showed no interest in making anything more involved than simple desserts. Surely Grandmother had tried to produce in my mother this same sense of responsibility for delicious meals for the family. Nevertheless, I was proud that Grandmother thought me worthy of instruction, and silently promised not to let her down.

"Let me look at your school work in the parlor when you're through, Jewell," Grandmother said, as she refastened a large tortoise shell hairpin into the soft bun of dark hair on the back of her head. Satisfied that meal preparations were proceeding well, she turned with a smile and walked back into the hall.

I spied the special mixing bowl, a small amount of dough still clinging to its inside. With my fingers I swiftly lifted the dough out and into my mouth. Raw dough, what a delight! I loved it so! I could taste the developing flavor of those exquisite rolls that would be served later. Even as I ran my fingers around the bowl, I did so with reverence.

Usually I would eat a lot of dough, as much as would have made two or three rolls for baking. Lillian would caution me against eating too much, so as not to spoil my supper. But for me, eating dough nourished my spirit as much as my body.

Later, at suppertime, when the browned and glazed rolls appeared in the linen-covered bowl on the table, it seemed a marvel to my seven-year old mind. With each delicious, butter-soaked bite, I tasted the essence of the yeast, of Lillian, and of love.

Even my beloved grandfather admitted to me one evening after dinner, "When I pray, 'Give us this day our daily bread'—frankly, I'm thinkin' of Lillian's yeast rolls."

# 26 | Smoke, Smoke, Smoke That Cigarette

MY MOTHER, MABEL, WAS AN impressionable teen when the flapper era began. She did her best to fit the model of a progressive young woman. One picture of her shows an attractive, slender girl with dark, bobbed hair wearing a one-piece bathing suit with a diamond patterned short skirt and solid top. One arm is jauntily cocked on her right hip and the other holds an opened Japanese paper parasol, a pose considered very stylish at the time.

Mother's younger sister, Thelma, was the true flapper in the family, always just a eyelash away from getting into real trouble. Mother was outspoken in her disapproval of many of Thelma's antics, but tried to keep up with her on the fashion front. Smoking for women was really in fashion, so both Thelma and Mabel enthusiastically participated.

Grandmother Creed was appalled at her daughters' short skirts and low necklines and willingness to "go along with the crowd." She especially hated to see the girls smoking, and told them so at every opportunity.

"It's a nasty habit and not fittin' for proper young ladies. I thought I reared you better than that."

Chafing under any and all restrictions and bored with small town life, Thelma married young and moved out of town, leaving Mabel as the focus of Grandmother's surveillance and reproach.

Mother married when she was twenty-two, and her husband, Roland, put his Lucky Strikes next to her Chesterfields on the bedside table.

By the time I was born, Grandmother had reluctantly accepted that Mabel and her cigarettes were unlikely to be parted. But as I began to grow up and ask questions about smoking, Grandmother devised a plan of action that she hoped would shame my mother into quitting.

Beginning when I was four years old my assistance was solicited for the project. Every Saturday afternoon Grandmother would hand me a brown paper sack. I would follow Grandmother as she checked every room in the house for ashtrays. She would pick up the containers and, holding them at arms length, dump the cigarette butts and ashes into the paper sack which I proudly held open for her.

"Ooh—doesn't that smell terrible, Jewell? I don't know how your mother can stand it," Grandmother grumbled as she emptied each ashtray.

I would try to match my Grandmother's screwed-up nose and frown. "Ooh—it smells terrible! I don't know how Mother can stand it," I would declare, tossing my long dark curls from side to side.

As Grandmother dumped each ashtray's contents into the bag, she would cough loudly as clouds of ashes rose from the tumbling butts. Soon I was frowning and coughing even more dramatically as the ashtrays were picked up and the repulsive residue poured into the sack.

When Mother came home from work each Saturday, Grandmother and I would present her with the sack full of smelly butts and ashes. Emboldened by being Grandmother's ally, I would cough loudly several times for effect.

With wide eyes and flaring nostrils Grandmother would fling out the weekly challenge. "Here, Mabel, look at this disgustin' mess. How in the world you can stand to smoke is beyond me. What a terrible example you're settin' for your own chile!"

Fortunately for me, it was Grandmother's example that endured. I have never even taken a puff off a cigarette. Grandmother's endeavor produced an aversion in me that saved me a lot of money over the years, not to mention helping to keep me healthy.

My mother never quit smoking. Why would she? Full color ads showed doctors in white coats instructing, "Smoke Pall Malls—for a smoother taste and a healthier draw." Her favorite movie actresses, Veronica Lake and Claudette Colbert, smiled down from the movie screen, lipstick-stained cigarettes dangling languorously from their lips.

Mother was chain-smoking three packs a day when she died at 62 years old.

Jewell and Aunt Bea at the country club pool

A pint-sized Jewell with the beautiful chow, "Ming Toy."

# 27 | *My Real Aunt Bea —*
*"Mercy Me!"*

I HAD A HARD TIME SLEEPING that April night. Aunt Bea had arrived that afternoon triggering a flurry of enthusiastic activity on the part of everyone in the family, with the notable exception of my mother, Mabel.

I had caught snatches of conversation over the years about how Thelma, Bea's baptized name, had deliberately stolen her friend's fiance, and married him herself in order to escape from Mount Airy's small town life. Grandmother said she was now living in Columbus, Ga. and her husband was "doing very well."

My mother didn't talk much about her, but I did remember hearing her say something to the effect that Thelma got by with everything, while she, the older and more dependable daughter, was left to work in the family book store and take up the slack. I wondered why she was now called Bea instead of Thelma and thought that I would ask my Grandmother about that sometime.

As soon as I saw her, I knew she was special. Her red hair was twisted into a soft roll on the back of her head, and she was wearing a smart navy and white striped two- piece dress, with a white jabot at the neck. A high-crowned, brimmed navy hat, large white earrings and navy and white spectator pumps completed the outfit.

She definitely had an out-of-town look. Her appearance was very regal, and she seemed taller than anyone else in the family.

Turning a bright smile in my direction she said, "Hello, Jewell, I'm your Aunt Bea." After I had muttered a responsive hello, she continued "Well, mercy me! What a lovely young lady you've turned out to be, Jewell. Tell you what, tomorrow we'll do something special. Put on a Sunday dress and meet me at the foot of the stairs after lunch."

Later, when I excitedly told my mother of the conversation, she mumbled, "Isn't that just like Thelma—soon as she gets here she starts to take over everything and everybody."

The next day I barely touched my food—having no interest in anything until the promised time with my aunt. When the hour arrived, I stood at the base of the stairs, wearing a blue and white organza dress with daisies on it and a large white bow in the back. My black patent dress shoes completed the Sunday-go-to-meeting look.

Aunt Bea appeared, her red hair now loosened and flowing. She wore green dangling earrings that matched her green and white silk dress. The dress barely covered her knees, and I couldn't help but notice what pretty legs she had as she took my hand and led me up the mahogany stairs.

Turning at the top of the stairs and to the left, she led me into the room that was sometimes referred to as the Sleeping Room, and sometimes as the Sun Porch. It had been closed all winter and Grandmother and Lillian had just finished opening it up last week. There were windows all around letting in the bright midday sun. The white cotton curtains were freshly washed and starched and their green ball trim matched the yellow and green covered white wicker couch and chairs. The day-bed had a white cover with bright pink day lilies on it and the whole room shouted with joy.

Aunt Bea opened two of the windows and fresh spring air flooded in. "Now," she said with a lilt in her voice, "It's time for us to have us a party." She took my hand and led me to the child-sized table and chairs where she had already set up the demitasse set she had sent me several months earlier for my sixth birthday. My mother had fussed about it being such an impractical gift for a young girl. But I loved it! It was real white china with pink roses encrusted on the pieces—a pot and four small cups and saucers. Small silver spoons were in place. Matching sugar and cream containers and a white china plate holding sugar cookies completed the setting, all placed on a pink linen tablecloth. As I sat down, Aunt Bea lowered herself onto the diminutive chair, stretching her long legs out to the side, and carefully arranging her dress around her. As we placed the pink linen napkins edged with tatting on our laps, she smiled and said, "We're going to have a passel of fun together, Jewell - just the two of us."

She began an elaborate ritual, carefully pouring the much weakened coffee first into my cup, and then hers. As she leaned forward, the smell of roses from her perfume drifted into my nostrils. She asked me to pour some cream from the pitcher into our cups. A generous helping of sugar was added, accompanied by instructions on just how to hold my hand and spoon in order to stir in a ladylike manner.

At her suggestion, we proceeded to have a very stylized conversation, in which I was addressed as "Miss Jewell," and she as "Miss Bea" as if we were equally grown-up ladies. There was a lot of giggling from both of us. In between the coffee and cookies, she talked with me, explaining how it was important to dress well, to have nice things and to act like a lady. There was a vibrancy in her voice, a sense of excitement with life. I was captivated by her. I loved her red hair, her finely chiseled features, her slender body and the willowy way I had seen her walk. It was a magical time and I was very happy.

As I reached for more cream, my hand slipped, and the white liquid spilled out onto the tablecloth. I recoiled from the scene, expecting a tongue-lashing for being so clumsy. Instead, Aunt Bea just said, "Mercy me! Come on, Jewell, grab the extra napkins and we'll get this cleaned up quickly." The liquid was soon absorbed, and she placed the wet napkins onto an extra plate at the side of the table. "Would you like some more, Miss Jewell," she asked, offering me another cookie, and, to my amazement, acting as if nothing had happened.

When we had finished the last drop and crumb of refreshment, Aunt Bea placed all the items on a tray and said, "Well, wasn't that fun! Thank you so much Miss Jewell for coming to my party." Turning she picked up the tray and started out the door. "Let's take all these things back down to the kitchen and I'll show you how to care for your demitasse set."

I followed her down the stairs, turning to the left down the hall and entering the kitchen. She placed the tray on the counter to the right and pulled over a green wooden step-stool in front of the sink. Walking over to the kitchen pantry, she opened the door and took a brightly flowered apron off a nail and put it over my head, tying the apron strings behind my back. "Okay, Jewell," she said, "get up on the stool and I'll show you what you need to know."

I got up on the stool, holding the front of the apron so as not to step on it. For the next half-hour, I was engrossed in Aunt Bea's careful instructions. How much hot water was to go in the left side of the sink and how much Ivory liquid was to be added to it. How to fill the right side of the sink with cool water for rinsing, and how to carefully place the pieces in the dish drain for drying with a linen towel later. I was so afraid I would somehow let a piece slip and break, but Aunt Bea kept assuring me that I would do very well and that there was nothing to fear. And I did do very well. All the pieces were washed and sparkling in the drain, with nary an accident.

When we finished, Aunt Bea made a curtsy in my direction and said, "Miss Jewell, it has been so good to visit with you this afternoon. Perhaps we will be able to do it again sometime."

I didn't want our time together to be over, but at Aunt Bea's direction, I went to find my mother in another part of the house so that Aunt Bea could "attend to some errands."

I walked very slowly, trying hard to hold on to the delight of that enchanted afternoon with my Aunt Bea.

# 28 | *Aunt Bea—Drinking in the Nectar of Life*

AUNT BEA CONTINUED TO BRING EXCITEMENT and glamour to my life, even after she went back to Georgia, I got letters from her frequently. They were always light and breezy with descriptions of the exciting trips she and her husband were taking, and all the things we could do together if my mother would let me come and visit them. She signed them, "With All My Love, Aunt Bea." I read them over and over.

Every time my mother's younger sister was spoken of in the family, she was referred to as "Thelma." When I asked Grandfather why the different names, he'd reply, "Now Jewell, you don't need to be worrying your pretty little head about things like that. I'm glad you and she get along so well together. Just enjoy your time with her, honey." He would give me one of those loving smiles that made him so dear to me, and then change the subject.

When I asked Grandmother the same question she would reply, "Ask me no questions and I'll tell you no lies." It was a favorite phrase of hers and was intended to stop any further conversation.

When I asked my mother, she rolled her eyes, flipped her head and replied, "Who knows the reason why Thelma does anything? She just does what she wants to. She wanted to leave Mount Airy and so she did. Left me to handle all the work at the Book Store. Even when she was here, she wouldn't show up to help half the time—some excuse or another. And Father always let her get by with it." The frown on her face and the resentment in her voice told me to drop the question!

Aunt Bea called my mother long distance from Georgia, just to beg her to let me spend the summer with her and Uncle Bill. Mother was strongly against the idea. I waited for the best moments to plead with her to let me go, trying not to "set her off" on another report of her sister's personality flaws.

One night I overhead Grandfather making his feelings on the matter clear to my mother. "Now Mabel, you know Jewell will be well cared for there. And besides, it'll give you some time to yourself, to go out with your friends. You know Ellen and I love having Jewell over here, but your mother and I are gettin' older, and she's a handful sometimes. It would give all of us a break."

Mother protested, "But Thelma is such a flibbertigibbet. No tellin' what ideas Jewell would pick up in a summer with her."

"Mabel," Grandfather said firmly, "Thelma is a grown woman now, and this time she's got a really good husband, a stable one. And whether you like it or not, it's obvious that she and Jewell get along famously. Let the chile go!"

In my prayers that night I gave a special blessing to Grandfather and begged God to let me spend the summer in the big city of Columbus, Georgia with Aunt Bea and Uncle Bill.

God heard my prayers. The first week of June, Mother and I began what would become a summer routine. We'd take a bus to Winston-Salem, board the Silver Meteor train there for the trip to Atlanta, Georgia and then on to Columbus.

Mother used the occasion to teach me the ways of fine dining. In the Dining Car, everything was "first class," with gloved waiters, many courses, and finger bowls. The train was such an exciting place for a young girl that I was reluctant to leave.

Mother visited her sister for a couple of days before returning home. It only took me a few hours to understand why they didn't get along. They had different ideas on everything! There were some tense moments, but not wanting to get into a big ruckus "in front of the chile" they kept their pot of grievances on simmer.

After Mother left, I began my enchanted time with Aunt Bea and Uncle Bill. Everything about their lives was different from anything I had ever experienced. Columbus had tall buildings and a big-city atmosphere. Aunt Bea and Uncle Bill lived at the Country Club in an apartment that overlooked the 8th tee of the golf course. I had never seen a golf course before. Uncle Bill played golf often so I would stand outside and watch for him to come to that spot and we would wave at each other before he moved on.

Uncle Bill was a big man, over 6 ft. and with a bulky frame. He could have been intimidating, but he had a soft voice and was one of the kindest men I would ever meet.

Aunt Bea and Uncle Bill didn't have any children, and while I was with them, they both treated me as if I were their daughter. I soaked up the attention Uncle Bill gave me. Until now, I had placed my need for a father figure on my Grandfather and I loved him dearly. But Uncle Bill was a man about the age of a real father and he talked to me and cared for me in the way I had dreamed a real father would.

When I asked Aunt Bea about how they had met, she admitted that it had been rather unconventional. Through the years I found out that that "unconventional" was Aunt Bea's middle name.

"Mercy me, honey, your mother doesn't even know that story. But the truth is, it was through a wrong number on the phone!" She giggled, the blush on her face matching her curly red hair. "But don't you ever do anything like that, you hear me? That was a simpler time. A gal's gotta be careful these days."

Glossing over the fact that she had agreed to meet a man she had only talked to on the phone, her description of their phone conversation gave me some clues. He had revealed that he had been a tackle with the famed Chicago Bears football team, during the time it was being led by the famous Red Grange. The allure of dating a professional football player with the accompanying aura of glamour, overcame any reservations about propriety; not that she had ever been much concerned about that, according to the tales mother had told about her younger years.

The summers with my aunt and uncle were wonderful. I had my own pass card for the Country Club pool and was invited to all the wonderful parties they and their friends threw at the Club. Everything was "first class" and they had loads of well-to-do friends, whose children became my friends. We took trips and went to concerts and plays. It was great!

It was a real bonus that they had a dog. I'm not sure why, but I had never had any pets, not at the apartment Mother and I shared or at my grandparents' house. Aunt Bea had a beautiful pedigreed Chinese Chow named "Ming Toy." Despite the chows' reputation, Ming Toy was the gentlest of dogs with me. I don't remember him ever growling at me, although he fiercely protected Aunt Bea when we were walking outside. When I was small I would try to ride him around the house. He would take it as long as he could and then slip out from under me and hide under the bed. I loved hugging him and rubbing my face against his soft fur.

I once asked Aunt Bea, "Did you buy Ming Toy because his hair is almost the same color as yours?"

She laughed and shook her red curls vigorously, "Well, mercy me! I didn't think of that at the time. But you know, we *are* both natural redheads!"

We spent long hours talking. She admitted that she had been somewhat of a rebel in her younger years. She told the story of how one Sunday her mother had surprised her as she was leaping and dancing to the music of a jazz band playing on the wind-up Victrola in the Parlor. Grandmother had a strong prohibition against dancing on Sundays, and tore into her about desecrating "The Lord's Day."

Aunt Bea had taken a deep breath and replied, in as innocent sounding a voice as she could muster, "Why Mother, whatever do you mean? I'm not dancing. I'm just exercising to music!" This ability to turn potential disaster into victory was a recurring theme in her life.

We were getting along so well that one day I had the courage to ask her, "Aunt Bea, why did you leave Mount Airy?"

"Mercy me! There were so many reasons. I'm a big city girl at heart. That little town couldn't hold me back. I just couldn't wait to get away. And I've never regretted it. Why, honey, they just aren't "with it."

You know, one time your Uncle Bill and I came home to visit and we were staying up at the Blue Ridge Hotel. It was the only decent place in town. We went to the dining room and ordered fried shrimp. The waiter didn't even know what it was - can you believe that? I found out later that they had it on the menu - but they didn't know the correct name. Would you believe it - they were calling the shrimp "little fishies!"

It seemed as good a time as any, so I took a deep breath and asked THE question that nobody else in the family seemed to want to answer. "Why do you call yourself "Aunt Bea" when the others at home call you "Thelma?"

There was a long pause and then she said, "Thelma is my Christian given name, but I never much cared for it. Bea is my name now, because I take the world's honey from so many different places. I like to check out everything, and take a little from here and a little from there." She paused and instructed, "Come on Jewell, we'll have lunch now."

As the years went by Aunt Bea and Uncle Bill continued to play a significant part in my life. She treated my children as if they were her grandchildren and lovingly interfered in all our lives. Aunt Bea lived to be 92 years old, and was spirited and strongly opinionated to the end.

## The Rest of the Story

Aunt Bea's explanation about her two different names satisfied me at the time. However, thinking about it over the years, it didn't make sense that family members were unwilling to give me an explanation that was that simple. Bits and pieces of the puzzle have come together during the ensuing years.

Thelma was so anxious to leave the small town she grew up in that she was willing to take bold steps to achieve her dreams. According to my mother (who may have colored the story somewhat) Thelma set her sights on a young man who had announced his intention to "get away from this hick town" and head to a big city.

The only problem was that the young man was engaged to Thelma's best friend. Thelma was, as they say, "quite a looker" and had been known to mesmerize young men with honey-dripping words, flickering eyelashes, and beautiful green eyes. It is said that the way to a man's heart is through his stomach, but somehow I felt that Aunt Bea had taken a different route.

I am not sure just how she accomplished it, but the next thing anybody knew, they had run away together to get married and start life anew. Her married name was Beaman, and somewhere along the way, she picked up the nickname "Bea."

Apparently everything went fairly smoothly in the marriage for the first year or two. Then one evening, when Bea was coming home from her job at a retail clothing store, everything changed. When she opened the closet door to hang up her coat, her husband jumped out of the closet, clad only in Bea's laciest bra and scanty underpants. Thelma had wanted a new and exciting life, but that was a little *too* much excitement even for her. A divorce quickly followed.

Never in all the years I knew her did she ever mention having been married before Uncle Bill, and even denied it when questioned directly.

"Why mercy me! What in the world would make you think a thing like that? Your sweet Uncle Bill is the only man I could ever love! Enough of this talk, let's go get an ice cream cone."

Aunt Bea lived life on her own terms. Mercy Me! We should all live as well.

# 29 | *Nuts and Spices*

PREPARATIONS FOR THE THANKSGIVING and Christmas holidays began early at Grandmother's house. Dark, rich, moist fruitcakes were made at the beginning of October. Large round pans were used for family cakes and loaf pans for gifts. Since I was designated to stir the batter with the big wooden spoon, my hands and arms would be quite tired and aching at the end of a day of baking duties. But I tried not to complain. It was an important part of a honored ritual.

"Mix it in better, Jewell. Make sure you can't see any flour," Grandmother instructed. All the flour, molasses, candied citron, cherries and pecans were folded in and stirred carefully until the mixture developed into an appropriately stiff batter.

Preparation for some of the ingredients was done even earlier in the year. When the pecan crop came in from the groves on her tenant farms, Grandmother, Mother, and I would sit down with a bucket full of pecans, armed with nutcrackers and shiny picks ready for action. We cracked the pecan shells carefully in order to get the pecan halves out whole for fruitcakes and other fancy baked goods. The crisp, aromatic halves were carefully put in a covered glass jar and saved for their divine purposes. Any broken pieces were put in another container to be used in candy, brownies, and other baking that didn't require the perfection of intact halves.

A dozen or so fruitcakes were made in the course of a day. The delicious aroma of fruit and spices permeated the entire house, and wafted out the kitchen windows, alerting the neighborhood to the delights within. It was not surprising that the other children on the street chose this time to come over to see if I could come out to play.

Grandmother always refused the request, explaining, "Jewell can't come out now—she's helpin' with the baking." I would swell with pride at her words. I could play anytime - being trusted to help Grandmother was much more important. However, each neighbor child would be allowed to linger in the kitchen long enough to go away with at least one piece of cake that "didn't come out quite right."

When the cakes were removed from the oven, Grandmother placed fresh cut apple slices around the outsides and into the center holes. Honey-glazed and cooled, they were then wrapped in wax paper and placed in various cake tins and other containers for storage in the cellar underneath the house. "They need time for the flavors to marry," Grandmother stated, her voice resonating with years of experience.

By the time Thanksgiving came 'round, the apple slices had fermented and the juices and flavor seeped into the fruitcakes, giving them a tinge of alcohol not otherwise permitted in Grandmother's teetoataling household.

Other designated baking days would produce additional goodies, among them banana nut bread, apple and prune loaves, and pumpkin spice bread. One of my favorites was a black walnut bread, although I certainly didn't relish the preparations for it. The walnuts came from a very large tree outside the back porch door. Mother Nature had devised an effective protection for the tree's delicious product. First was a tough covering of black and green, almost like leather. Touching it immediately produced a stain on the fingers and on anything else they subsequently touched. Consequently, the effort to harvest the delicious meat of this nut was relegated to the backyard.

Once its external guarding peel was removed, wearing pairs of Grandmother's old gardening gloves to protect our hands, the second layer of protection was exposed—an extremely hard and rough black shell. No nutcrackers were up to this task. We would place each shell on the concrete sidewalk and, holding it tightly with the left hand, use a sturdy hammer to strike it with the right hand. I was less than skillful at this task, and had a number of bruised fingers to attest to my inadequacies.

One year, a great idea came to me, and saved me from further embarrassment and pain. Placing my small red wooden chair on the sidewalk, I pulled the bucket of fresh black walnuts to my side and took my place on the chair. One by one, I placed those rough, hard-shelled nuts between my two feet, being careful to wear old, but sturdy, shoes. Using my feet as a vise, I pounded away until each shell split open and gave up its bounty.

Occasionally, Grandfather was enlisted for this important project. I watched in awe as he broke open each black walnut swiftly with a single blow of his hammer. My job was to quickly pick the nut sections up and put them in a bucket so the women could remove their contents later.

There was no effort by any of the participants in these violent nut-killing scenes to keep the black walnut meat unbroken. Pieces of black walnuts were just fine for cakes, breads and dark, delicious fudge.

Each time I began to tire, I kept my efforts going by anticipating enjoying delicious black walnut bread, warm, sweet and freshly buttered, together with my mother's special hot, spiced tea.

## TAGS *Notes:*

Episode

#87    "Aunt Bee's Medicine Man"
Andy says that Aunt Bee is a real "teetotaler." She won't even allow fruitcake in the house because of problems her brother had.

❖    My mother prided herself on her spiced tea recipe. It was hot, strongly-brewed black pecoe tea with the addition of orange and pineapple juices and cloves, simmered for "just the right amount of time." She called it "Russian Tea," and served it for all the ladies' bridge functions, together with white bread sandwiches carefully cut in the shapes of clubs, diamonds, hearts and spades.

Imagine my surprise many years later, when I was living in the Kingdom of Saudi Arabia, when a Middle Eastern friend of mine served a tea made by the exact same recipe, proudly describing it as "my mother's special recipe for Sudanese Tea."

❖    While I was growing up, Grandmother was adamant that "no store-bought fruitcake is as good as homemade." However, in the mid 1940's when a Kroger supermarket opened in Mount Airy, and my grandmother was pushing 80, she told everybody that she had tasted Kroger's fruitcake and it would be satisfactory. Her Holiday Baking Spoon was retired and we purchased our fruitcakes from that time on.

# 30 | Grandmother's Gift

"PLEASE TELL MABEL TO LET ME GO. It's my time and I'm ready." The voice of my grandmother pleaded with me to intercede and let her die peacefully.

Mabel was my mother and just minutes before, with panic in her voice, she had wakened me. "Grandma's dying—stay with her while I get help!" Ignoring the telephone at hand, mother had gone next door to get help from the neighbors and have them call an ambulance.

For all of my thirteen years, my grandmother had been much closer to me than my own mother. Grandmother was a rugged matriarch, and I had great respect for the way she had kept her family running in the '30's and '40's. She passed some of her knowledge on to me, teaching me indispensable homemaking skills by both word and example. Many times she had guided me as I stood on a the kitchen stool, stirring with the long-handled wooden spoon, tending to my skimming duties, as together we made pear preserves from the fruit of the tree in the backyard. Just that day, at 82 years old, she had supervised the workmen on the roof of the house, using her strong voice and a cane to direct their actions.

Even so, I did not realize at that time what a significant effect the minutes that followed would have on my entire life.

I had rushed into her bedroom to find my beloved grandmother lying upon the bed, her dark, waist-long hair streaming over the pillows. "It's okay, Jewell, it's my time and I'm ready to move on," she announced. Her demeanor was so matter-of-fact and her voice so calm that I felt no fear, but rather an ordinariness about what was happening.

She was quiet for a minute, her eyes closed. "Jewell, are you there?"

"I'm here, Grandmother."

"Good," she replied. "You know, it's not so bad."

I didn't really know what to say, so I said something really dumb, "Are you dying, Grandmother?"

"I guess that's what they call it," she said, "but it feels really right." Casually, she began an amazing narrative. "Jewell, I see so many wonderful things."

"What kind of things?"

"There are so many trees and flowers. I've never seen those kinds of trees before; I don't even know what they are. And the flowers—they're beautiful—but I've never seen anything like them before either."

This from a master green-thumb gardener, who must have had at least a hundred varieties of flowers and plants growing on her property. We never needed to go to a florist. Grandmother grew lilies of the valley, fern, roses -everything needed for a corsage. When I asked her why she planted so many varieties, she would answered, "Just to prove I can grow them."

"What colors are the flowers?" I asked.

"Green, blue, gold—and lots of other colors I've never seen before," she replied.

Abruptly Grandmother switched from physical details to information about people.

"Oh, there's cousin Ben—it's good to see him — and Mary and John, Mary's husband. They look so happy." Grandmother smiled and fell silent for a minute.

"I see Eloise and Samuel, and Betty Sue and—" The recitation stopped abruptly. Then she continued in an even stronger voice, "My goodness—there's Mazie. Her smile turned into a frown. No—I can't believe that she's here, and I don't want talk about it." Mazie was a long-dead cousin of my grandmother's that I had not heard spoken of in any positive manner.

Suddenly, Grandmother's eyes lit up, the smile returned to her face and she exclaimed, "Oh Jewell, you would love the music. It is really beautiful!"

I had begun singing at age 4 and had joined every choral group possible through the years, with my grandmother encouraging me all the way. Now I felt she was giving me assurance that any talents I possessed would be useful eternally.

With the audacity that only a teenager can have, I continued to ask her questions. "Who else do you see?" She replied with names of people who were unfamiliar to me, along with some I recognized as those I had been told had died before I was born. "What do the they look like?"

"They're more beautiful than I remember them," she replied.

All of a sudden a wave of sadness rolled over me as I became aware that I might lose forever the loving interaction we had always had. I had been privy to the secret that Grandmother had a 'bad heart' and knew that the doctor's pronouncement had been kept from her. But it had been almost five years since I had first heard the whispered concerns, and she had always seemed invincible to me.

"How do you feel?" I asked, my voice quivering.

She sighed, and then in a clear, strong voice said, "Jewell, I feel I belong there now and I'm ready to cross over."

Just then, my mother returned, flushed and out of breath, to announce that the ambulance was on its way. Grandmother smiled and said, "That's nice, Mabel, but I won't be needing it."

With those words she closed her eyes and quietly made her transition to the 'other side.'

Grandmother's gift to me that night was the most important legacy I have ever received. Since that time, I have felt a strong sense of peace, sure in the knowledge that life does not die—it just goes on in another dimension.

When some doctors talk about death they theorize that chemical changes in the brain produce spontaneous 'visions.' They may believe that explanation, but in the case of my grandmother's passing, I know better. There was an interchange of questions and answers that covered at least ten minutes. She was fully rational, laughing at some of my questions, and expressing astonishment at much of what she was seeing.

I am convinced that life is eternal, and, thanks to Grandmother, I plan to live every moment of it fully—both here and hereafter.

# Keeping Mayberry Alive

Mount Airy Visitors Information Center, 708 N. Main St.

"The hypnotic tranquility of Mayberry - America's favorite small Southern town—has inspired an ever-increasing band of devotees who are flocking by the thousand to Mount Airy, the place they call 'the real Mayberry.'"                              — *Atlanta Journal Constitution*

"Mount Airy is reminiscent of a simpler time, when life moved a little slower and people knew their neighbors . . . It's comforting to know places such as Mount Airy still exist in America and they warmly welcome visitors."                              — *The Dallas Morning News*

"As *The Mayberry Confidential* says: 'Mayberry is that wonderful mind set for each of us where wrongs are righted, the food is all home-cooked, life is simple, the rocking chairs are waiting on the porch and, best of all, people are welcomed and made to feel at home when they visit.' The newsletter may mean Mayberry, but it sounds just like Mount Airy."                              — *The Miami Herald*

Emmett Forrest at the Andy Griffith Playhouse for a
"Mayberry Days" presentation by "The Dillards," a.k.a.
"The Darlings"— (Looks like Otis is attending too!)

# 31 | *Emmett—Fixin' Andy in Time*

> *"Make new friends, but keep the old—one is silver, the other is gold"*
>
> — Traditional

FOR ANDY GRIFFITH, EMMETT FORREST certainly is in the gold category. In boyhood days, they played "kick the can" from the street light at Rockford and Broad down to Haymore Street where Andy lived. Today, Andy Griffith is one of the most recognized and beloved television stars, and Emmett is still faithful to their friendship.

The popularity of Sheriff Andy Taylor—a character which drew significantly from Andy Griffith's own personality and background—has produced a groundswell of caring by myriads of fans. More than 40 years since *The Andy Griffith Show* first aired on television, episode reruns attract more viewers than any other comedy series. Devotees of the show, with it's homespun humor and clearly-defined values, still seek connections to Andy, *Mayberry*, and simpler times.

As one of the biggest of those fans, Emmett Forrest helps keep the memories alive. The Andy Griffith Museum in the Visitors Information Center in Mount Airy contains the largest collection of Andy Griffith memorabilia in the country. There is everything from the chair Andy was rocked in as a baby to a suit he wore on *Matlock*.

The Museum is not the result of Andy Griffith's desire for immortality. In fact, Andy has never seemed comfortable with the trappings of celebrity, or the adulation of the crowds, opting instead to be a very private person and let his work speak for him. Virtually all of the items in the collection have been painstakingly acquired by Emmett and are displayed as a tribute to Andy.

When asked about the time, money and effort involved in acquiring the contents for the Museum, Emmett responds with a nostalgic smile. "It's just something I wanted to do," he explains modestly. "Andy and I came from the same working-class background and experienced both the challenges and the freedom that exist in a small town. We didn't have much money, so we learned to make the best of what we had. My memories of the time we spent together bring me pleasure. I'm very proud of what Andy has accomplished." Unmistakable affection flows out with Emmett's soft southern voice.

Emmett and Andy still keep in touch. As Sheriff Andy Taylor put it, "No matter where life takes you, you always carry in your heart the memories of old times and old friends." Sometimes recollections of growing up together in the small mountain town are the focus of their conversations. They reflect on the years of their youth when they walked together to Rockford Street Grammar School, and where recess was a favorite subject. At lunch time, they usually brought something from home; although Andy had been known to head up Main Street to the Snappy Lunch for a 5 cent bologna sandwich and a bottle of Orange Crush. Any extra change might have been spent on a Moon Pie or Goo-Goos.

Times change, but true friends remain. We all owe Emmett Forrest a debt of gratitude for his caring nature and continuing focus on the significant role Andy Griffith and Mayberry have played in so many lives. As the TV reporter on "Entertainment Tonight" put it:

"Andy Griffith is our most endearing and enduring entertainer."

## TAGS *Notes:*

Episode

# 32  "Bringing Up Opie"
Opie plays "kick the can" all over town

# 44  "Sheriff Barney"
Barney walks down the street kicking a can

#159  "Banjo Playing Deputy"
Is school crossing guard on the corner of Haymore and Rockford

Charles Dowell, Owner of the Snappy Lunch, serves up his famous Pork Chop Sandwich.

"It takes more than a glorified pork chop in a hamburger bun to generate the kind of allure radiated by this tiny diner on Main Street. Snappy Lunch serves each of its customers a generous helping of small-town America—and that is a tasty dish that's getting mighty hard to find."

— *Gourmet*

# 32 | *The Snappy Lunch*

AS I GOT OUT OF MY CAR in the parking lot, I smelled the delicious aroma of food cooking at the Snappy Lunch. It smelled just like it did when I was a little girl going there with my grandfather.

When you open the screen door at the place, you step back in time. There is a simple menu, no frills, low prices and an open, welcoming atmosphere. Yes-siree, this is the famous Snappy Lunch.

It wasn't famous when I used to eat there with my grandfather. Well, actually it *was* famous with all the townspeople of Mount Airy and the surrounding area. The restaurant began serving its delicious offerings in 1923, and when I went there in the 1940's, it was *the* place to eat breakfast or lunch.

George Roberson, who was one of Grandfather's neighbors on Church Street, was one of the original owners, and my grandfather took every opportunity to support his friend's business. Not that it took much effort; the food was delicious and the conversation enlightening.

In the beginning, patrons stood at the counter to eat. When I was going there with Grandfather, they had added stools at the counter, and a few high school desks for seating. I would slide into one of the desks to eat my juicy hot dog while my grandfather "chewed the fat" with Mr. Roberson. In those days they had sandwiches for 5 and 10 cents, and nothing was over 20 cents.

All those memories came flooding back as I settled into a seat at the Snappy Lunch recently. The establishment now had seating for 40 people, having taken over the adjacent Fant's Shoe Repair, adding booths in that area.

Andy Griffith remembered his time at the Snappy Lunch also, and mentioned it on *The Andy Griffith Show,* spreading its reputation for good food and good conversation far and wide. There are many interesting pictures on the walls, but two caught my particular attention. The first was of Charles Dowell, the owner and Oprah Winfrey; the second was of the naked back of a rabid fan who had all the major characters on the show *tattooed* on his back.

The Snappy Lunch is busy virtually all of the time from its opening at 6 a.m. to the 2 p.m closing time. You're more likely to encounter local people at breakfast. They've pretty well given up being able to eat in the place at lunch time, settling for calling in their orders for "take out."

The day I ate lunch there there was a big bunch of people standing at the front waiting for their orders, and the waitresses seemed to know them all personally.

"Bob, your order for 19 tenderloin biskits is ready," Dorothy called out.

Bob moved to the front of the group of about 15 people waiting for similar orders. Some of the orders were breakfast items with a twist: "I got 7 sausage sandwiches with tomato and mayo—I think that's yours, Elmer."

The Snappy Lunch is owned by Charles Dowell, who began working there in 1943, sweeping and cleaning up in the place. My conversation with him revealed many of the reasons, in addition to good food, that the place is so popular.

"We served white bread when we opened and we serve white bread now. Why mess with anything else? Keepin' it simple is part of the secret, and simple is what I grew up with," Charles explained.

For all of us who have seen the huge tractor trailer trucks pull up to our favorite restaurants and unload the pre-processed food ingredients to be used in the restaurant's meals, you will be interested in the way the Snappy Lunch prepares its food.

"We make all our own chili—our own slaw—our own batter. Nothing we serve is processed anywhere else. We do it ourselves. They bring in the raw meat we cut and batter the pieces."

For a number of years now, the Snappy Lunch has been famous for its pork chop sandwich. You can get it regular or "all the way." When I asked what "all the way" meant, Charles looked at the waitress and said, "Go ahead, Dorothy, tell her what it means—it won't make any difference, she'll order it 'all the way.'" I did—the statistics are that 99 out of 100 order it that way. (It includes tomato, onion, mustard, chili, and slaw, and produces a sandwich which is very difficult to handle and impossible to eat daintily—but who cares?)

Charles asked a sign maker to craft a sign saying that they served a pork chop sandwich to put on the outside of the restaurant. When the sign arrived, it said, "Home of the Famous Pork Chop Sandwich."

Charles said, "I told him I wish he hadn't done that, because it looked like I was braggin' and that ain't seemly."

"That very week a North Carolina television station came to do a story on the Snappy Lunch and they zoomed in on that sign, and once the story ran, it created a great demand. What really put us over the top was when the people from the Oprah Winfrey Show came here and asked about the pork chop sandwich, and it got mentioned on her show. They really put us on the map."

Also, it's not every day a pork chop sandwich gets written up in *Gourmet* Magazine. On an ordinary day, at least 200 pork chop sandwiches are sold, and many, many more during "Mayberry Days." At $2.50, the pork shop sandwich is the most expensive thing on the lunch menu. Charles is very proud of his affordable prices.

"You don't see other eating places with these kind of prices. I know I could get more; there's no doubt that I could almost double my prices and they'd still keep coming. But that's not the right way.

I like to see people happy. I think one of the things I was impressed with growing up was that in this town people try to help each other, not take advantage of each other."

He's certainly right about the prices. At the Snappy Lunch a family of four, all eating cheeseburgers, chugging down sodas and sharing two packages of potato chips, would owe a grand total of $9.70. Take that McDonalds!

You won't find dessert on the menu, but if you must have something sweet to finish your lunch, you can choose from individual servings of goodies displayed in the original Lance boxes used for shipping. You could choose cookies, small pecan or chess pies or a "Fat Free Fig Cake."

When asked what he liked best about his job, Charles replied, "The most fun part of the job is seeing people you'd never see otherwise, listening to them, seeing them laughing together—how excited they are to be here—helping them reconnect with the past."

They don't call it "Snappy Lunch" for nothing. The food is served hot and quick; true fast food with an "all the time in the world" feeling for the customer. In spite of lines out the door, no one is ever rushed. Here people really *are* more important that profits.

The Snappy Lunch is fast, frugal and fantastic. If you're up Mount Airy way, come on in—the people are friendly and the vittles are great!

## TAGS *Notes:*

Episode

#9    "Andy, the Matchmaker"
      Andy says that the Snappy Lunch is one of his favorite places to eat.

# Mount Airy Today

Andy Griffith's Childhood Home at 711 Haymore Street.

Old Earle Theater at 142 N. Main Street—now "Cinema" premiered "A Face in the Crowd."

# Mount Airy Today

Rockford Street School Auditorium at 218 Rockford Street—now the "Andy Griffith Playhouse."

Grace Moravian Church at 401 N. Main Street. Andy played in the band.

# The Super Snappy Lunch

It's worth the wait to enjoy a friendly meal at Snappy Lunch.

Eat in or take out at the Snappy Lunch.

# Barber Shop Memories

A visit to Floyd's City Barber Shop: a very patient customer waits
his turn between Russell's picture-taking sessions with visitors.

Russell says this old-fashioned cash register was in the barber shop
when he came to work 55 years ago. It's not just for show—all
transactions are rung up on "The Green Machine."

# Mayberry Days

Members of the "Who's Been Messing Up The Bulletin Board" Internet Chapter of the Rerun Watchers Club, with their leader, Allan "Floyd" Newsome, at left.

David Browning, appearing as "The Mayberry Deputy" rides an ox (okay, it's a Texas longhorn) in the parade. He said that Otis was too drunk to ride.

# Mayberry Days

Large crowds enjoy the many festivities, food and fun!

Not only is the quality of the bar-b-que judged, but also the best decorated entries. Check this one out!

# Hoedown Heaven

*Left:*
"Claw-hammer"
—banjo player supreme.

*Below:*
"The Professor,"
"Baby Blue," and a friend
give out the Gospel
message.

# Today in Mount Airy

U.S. Post Office in Mount Airy, made of local granite from the largest open-faced quarry in the world. Get a "Mayberry" postmark during "Mayberry Days."

Free Parking, well maintained and decorated lots, and easy access to popular sites, make Mount Airy a prime tourist designation. Many other interesting festivals take place all during the year.

# 33 | *Floyd's City Barber Shop*

THE CITY BARBER SHOP OPERATION dates back to 1929, when the phrase "shave and a haircut, 2 bits" was accurate. Even now, the City Barber Shop has some of the lowest prices in the state.

On *The Andy Griffith Show*, the barber shop was much more that a place of service for men's hair needs, it was a gathering point for political conversation, local gossip and "just getting together for spell." It was that way when I was growing up in Mount Airy, also. My grandfather stopped in to get his hair cut in that barber shop and I would sit and wait for him.

In 1946, Russell Hiatt came to work there as a barber and 55 years later he's still there. When Andy Griffith was home from college, he would drop by and get Russell to cut his hair, and Russell is proud to share his memories of those days.

"Looking back, I could see the seeds in him of his talent. He was pleasant, personable, an all-around nice guy. I'm happy to have had the opportunity to be of service to him."

When asked what has been the highlight of his years, Russell said, "Well, I tell ya—the most enjoyable thing about it is seeing all these people come in from all over the world. And I've always enjoyed my work."

The last time I was there I asked Russell if he knew how many haircuts he had given in his many years on the job. He indicated that he hadn't kept count, and a customer who was waiting for a turn chimed in, "There'd been a lot more if you didn't get so many interruptions!"

And interruptions there are. Ever since Floyd's City Barber Shop got so much publicity on *The Andy Griffith Show,* hardly a day goes by that some out-of-town fan doesn't comes into the shop and want his hair cut. Then there are those that just want to see the place and get their picture taken by "Floyd." Russell has nearly 20,000 Polaroid photos on his walls and he's never too busy to stop and let a visitor take his picture. Because of television's focus on the barber shop, the name on the window now reads: Floyd's City Barber Shop

When I asked him how he handled the "Mayberry Days"crowds, he indicated that the people line up outside his place and the Snappy Lunch next door and go into whatever establishment can take them first.

People come in from all over the world. Parents come from hundreds of miles away just to get their son's first haircut from Russell, and he has a special child-sized barber chair just for them. Tourists have been known to spend the night just to be at the barber shop first thing in the morning to get their hair cut. Russell answers to "Floyd" as easily as his real name.

Russell has a picture on the wall of Oprah Winfrey and himself when she and her crew came to film. He has also been featured on *The Today Show* and *Current Affairs.*

While he obviously is proud of those events, it doesn't seem to have changed his personality in any way.

When asked when he plans to retire, Russell says he has no plans for that: "I'm gonna stay around as long as my health is good enough for me to work."

Looking at Russell now, you would never suspect how seriously ill he was just a few years ago. He had a severe fall that left him perilously close to death. The doctors told the family he probably wouldn't live, but if he did, he would be brain dead. Defying all the odds, Russell recovered in five months.

When you are in Mount Airy, drop in to see Russell, also known as Floyd, in the City Barber Shop. You'll get as cordial a welcome as anywhere on the planet. He's a genuine person in a genuinely friendly town.

## TAGS *Notes:*

Episode

#9   "Stranger In Town"
     The character of Floyd, the barber, is introduced in this episode. Howard McNear's portrayal of Floyd is the image most fans have of the character. Mr. McNear bore little physical resemblance to Russell Hiatt, who many people feel inspired the idea of having the barber and the barber shop as an intregal part of life in *Mayberry*. However, in Episode 9, when the character of Floyd, the barber, was introduced it was played by Walter Baldwin, whose physical make-up is similar to Russell Hiatt's, and whose low-key portrayal of the barber was more like Russell's style. Television being what it is, it was decided that a more eccentric character was needed, and so McNear's comedic talents took over the part.

❧   On the wall in the real Floyd's City Barber Shop in Mount Airy is a plaque which reads:

     "The man who walks with God always gets to his destination."

"I always did want to be a barber, even when I was a little kid. I used to practice on cats. I'd catch them in the alley and then clip them. We had the baldest cats in the county."

—Floyd Lawson
The Barber

# 34 | *Hoedown Heaven*

THE WAIL OF A BOW BEING DRAWN across a fiddle. The twang of gee-tar string. The plunk-plunk of a banjo. These are the joyous sounds of mountain music.

The North Carolina mountain area around Mount Airy has long valued its music. All us young'uns were exposed to traditional music at an early age. Add to that the prevalence of inspirational gospel music in the area and you can understand why music both soothes us and spurs us on.

Andy Griffith had music in his soul at an early age. He heard gospel music in his home and over the radio, and the time he spent in the Moravian Church Band was, by his own account, a very positive experience in his teen years. So it is not surprising that he included both bluegrass and gospel sounds in *The Andy Griffith Show*. During the first year of the show, he featured a real-life group, "The Country Boys." Later, "The Darlings" were introduced and became a major part of the show. The non-speaking Darling boys were portrayed by the real music group, "The Dillards."

Fortunately that same kind of music is alive and well in Mount Airy today. On any Thursday evening, you can come to "The Andy

Griffith Playhouse" and experience "a-picking and a-grinning." and perhaps see some fancy footwork as well.

The last time I was there there were about fifteen local musicians, many carrying more than one instrument, performing a variety of crowd-pleasing pieces. Guitars, fiddles, banjos, mandolins, harmonicas, acoustic bass, and strong gospel and country singers—all joined together for a real "hoedown" to the delight of a room-filling crowd of people from all walks of life. The artists were randomly called upon by a young musician named Tim Chadwick, who acted as emcee for the evening. He had given each of the participants a nickname, such as calling the woman with the mandolin, Margaret "Boil That Cabbage Down" Eaton, in honor of one of her favorite pieces. His handling of the customized introductions for the three-hour session reminded me of the best of "Lake Wobegon."

A variety of talented individuals presented themselves to the assembled group of locals and tourists in a basement room of the Playhouse. When Andy and I were going to school here, this same area housed chorus practices for students at the Rockford Street Grammar School.

There was Rebecca "Baby" Blue, a short and firmly packed woman in her 70's with short-cropped white hair, who belted out "Life Is Like A Mountain Railroad," while holding a big black binder packed with a passel of song sheets. Then came John, a slender young man with a tuft of beard on his chin, who strummed his five-string blue grass banjo in a stirring rendition of "Blackberry Blossom," that belied the fact that he had been playing the instrument for only six months.

Tim announced the next number "in the key of G, for those scoring at home," and Clydus McTate, Archie Callahan and James "Rural" Hall joined in with the rest in a rousing rendition of "Healing on the Hallelujah Side."

During the course of the evening, all the musicians took part in the presentations. One would start a song, announcing the key being used, and one by one the rest of the group would come in. Solos on the various instruments were rotated by some invisible director, as each smoothly segued into the featured spot and out again into the background.

Occasionally, while the others were playing a rousing instrumental rendition of a favorite tune, Elbert Bronson, a small,wiry man with the nickname of "twinkle toes,"would take to the floor and begin to "flat foot" with gusto. I was worn out just watchin' him. He performed several times that night and, the next day at a "Mayberry Days" event was on the floor by himself or with a partner for virtually every number. When I interviewed him later, he shared the information that he had undergone heart by-pass surgery just a couple of years before. Let's hear it for mountain air and collard greens!

At one point, a young woman in her 20's came to the microphone and carefully placed her instrument under her chin. It was explained that she was a classical violinist who was in the area studying how to play the instrument as a "fiddle." During the break, I sought her out to discover what the differences were in producing the two very different sounds. She shared some technical information with me as to the placement of the fingers and use of the bow.

The next day, at the Surry County Regional Museum, I was to find an even better explanation. A violin bearing the mark of "Stradivarius" was on display. The accompanying sign indicated that many such violins were sold for $7 apiece from the Sears and Roebuck catalog in the late 1800's. The display featured this quote from a old mountain musician: "A fiddle plays 'Cacklin' Hen,' and a violin plays 'Der Flea and Der Mouse'."

During that Thursday evening session, my attention was drawn again and again to a very large, rotund man, nicknamed "Clawhammer," sitting on a chair up front, playing his banjo with abandon. His blue denim overalls were complemented with a red T-shirt, and his head sported a red baseball cap with a green and red plaid bill. With a long white beard flowing from his chin and beautiful green eyes that flashed a benevolent smile to all in the room, I felt sure that Santa Claus had joined us for the evening.

Toward the end of the session, the Warner Sisters took the center of the room. Born in the mid-west, but currently residents of the Carolina mountains, the three women were of very diverse body types, but unmistakably linked by their facial features. Their medley of perfectly harmonized gospel songs was enthusiastically received by everyone in the room, and they didn't seem to mind those of us who were singing along with them.

The audience also was delightfully diverse, including a number of tourists, some from far-away states, along with the local "regulars."Also enjoying the evening was a group of young people with Downs syndrome, who smiled and swayed with the rhythm of the music.

The evening was over far too soon. There is something about mountain music that is both mesmerizing and inspiring. Even now, the memory of the strings of the mandolins, banjos, and fiddles continues to pluck the strings of my heart.

## TAGS *Notes:*

Episode

#19    "Mayberry on Record"
       Andy and "The Country Boys" record a folk music album

#29    "Quiet Sam"
       The bluegrass group, "The Country Boys" appears again and Andy joins them in singing a rousing rendition of "She'll Be Comin' Round the Mountain"

#88    "The Darlings Are Coming"
       This musical mountain family is introduced, and delight us in a number of later episodes "The Dillards," the real bluegrass group playing the part, have appeared many times at the "Mayberry Days" celebration, along with Maggie Peterson Mancuso, who played Charlene Darling.

# 35 | WPAQ, the "Merry-Go-Round," and Andy Griffith

ON GROUNDHOG DAY IN 1948, residents of Mount Airy and the surrounding area tuned their radios to 740 on the AM dial to hear the first radio station in the area. No more depending on stations from the big cities of Winston-Salem, Greensboro or Charlotte. No siree, we now had our own station, WPAQ; and what a station it was—and IS!

The owner, Ralph Epperson, was committed to having a station that would showcase music and uplifting programs. Beginning with 78 rpm record music and "preachin' programs," the station was enthusiastically received by the area residents.

In that same year WPAQ started broadcasting, "The Merry-Go-Round," a lively bluegrass-gospel music hoedown on Saturdays. Local artists were joined occasionally by better-known names, including the legendary Bill Monroe. Today it is one of the longest-running programs of its kind in the country, and is broadcast every Saturday from the Cinema Theater on Main Street in Mount Airy. It's free to all, and everyone is encouraged to come in and "set a spell." But if your schedule doesn't permit that, never fear—the music is broadcast out onto Main Street so everybody can enjoy it.

Andy Griffith was already in college when Ralph started the station, but when he came back to visit or take part in local presentations, he would stop in the station to see Ralph. Andy was talented and obviously "on the way up" in the entertainment business, and so was sought after as a spokesman for non-profit groups. He was accommodating and generous, and came to the station to record public service announcement for a variety of causes.

One day Ralph received a 78 rpm demo record from Andy. He asked Ralph to listen to it and give him his opinion of it. Andy wanted to know if Ralph thought it was "worth making and playing, or should it just be thrown in the trash."

Ralph liked it and told Andy so. The title of the piece was, "What It Was, Was Football." After it began to air on WPAQ, other radio stations across the state started calling Ralph and wanting to know where they could get the record. When it started getting played by other stations, people across the state started asking where they could buy it. It was on an obscure label, and not easy to find. Capitol Records noticed the "buzz" about the piece and secured the rights to release it under the "Capitol" label. The rest is history. It remains one of the top comedy recordings of all time.

Over the years Ralph Epperson has been asked many times why he has not changed the format of the programs on WPAQ to be more in tune with "modern times."

"Why would we want to be like everybody else? The kind of music we play still strikes a responsive cord in people.

❖ Over the years, Andy Griffith has been very savvy about the value of commercials and endorsements. When he did a commercial for Orange Crush, he said that in "What It Was, Was Football," when he said "I'm gonna git myself a "big orange," he was referring to "Orange Crush."

❖ To learn more about WPAQ, and a CD featuring some country, bluegrass and gospel artists that appeared on the station through the years, contact: WPAQ, P. O. Box 907, Mount Airy, NC 27030 or call (336) 786-6111.

# 36 | "Mayberry Days" and More!

"IT WASN'T ANYTHING THAT WE ORIGINALLY planned, it just kinda happened. We appreciated the interest of the fans in our town and were just responding to their wishes." That's how Tanya Rees, Executive Director of the Surry Arts Council, explains how the arts group came to sponsor "Mayberry Days" in Mount Airy, North Carolina.

From the time *The Andy Griffith Show* debuted on television in 1960, fans who were aware that Mount Airy was Andy's hometown would drop by from time to time to seek out the real people and places that might have influenced the show. In the 1980's, following the publication of books and articles specifically linking the two towns, fans began coming to Mount Airy in increasing numbers. In the beginning, local folks just pitched in and helped the people find their way around, adding in information about the town in general. Soon, the people were coming in bus loads, looking for Andy, Opie, Barney and the rest of the *Mayberry* gang.

In 1990, the Surry Arts Council, with the cooperation of the Chamber of Commerce and the Visitors Center, decided to throw a giant party in honor of the 30th anniversary of *The Andy Griffith Show's* debut on television. And so "Mayberry Days" was born, featuring some of the actors that played on the show, writers and directors, character portrayers, a parade and other events reminiscent of TAGS. The three-day event is broadcast in its entirety by WPAQ.

The first year's effort was such a hit that "Mayberry Days" has become a permanent fixture each year on the last weekend in September. Each year both the activities and the crowds have increased as word spread about the event. In September of 2000, the registration books at the Visitors Center were signed by 5,000 visitors. Who knows how many others were wandering around town and never got around to signing the official register.

Frequently highlighting the event are concerts by "The Dillards," who performed on the the TV show as "The Darlings," with Maggie Peterson Mancuso reprising her role as Charlene Darling. Interactive events include contests for bar-b-que cooking, pie eating, horseshoe pitching and TAGS trivia. A myriad of other down-home activities keep the attendees happy, satisfied, and coming back year after year. Mount Airy citizens are as friendly as their television counterparts, and the town provides convenient free parking.

A good place to start your exploration at any time is The Visitors Information Center. Funded by the Gilmer-Smith Foundation, it houses many interesting items, including a significant collection of Andy Griffith memorabilia, pictures and information on the Siamese Twins and other information concerning the area. Ann Vaughn, Executive Director, oversees the operation of the Center. Attractive, vivacious, and highly knowledgeable, Ann communicates enthusiasm to all who come in contact with her.

Plan to come early or stay after "Mayberry Days" in order to take in some of the other attractions in the Mount Airy area. One is the world's largest open face granite quarry, where the black-speckled stone has been mined since 1889, and was used in prominent buildings throughout the nation. In recent years, the Museum of Regional History has opened with a variety of information and exhibits that illuminate the history and customs of the area, all very creatively displayed. There are many more things to see and do, and an inquiry to any of the sources mentioned below will elicit a prompt response.

Come visit for a spell and experience the meaning of:
"Mount Airy: Mountains, Music, *Mayberry* & More"

❖ For further information on the town of Mount Airy, "Mayberry Days,"or other area attractions, contact:

Mount Airy Visitors Center
615 North Main Street
Mount Airy, N. C. 27030
Toll Free 1-800-576-0231
E-Mail: visitandy@tcia.net

Mount Airy Chamber of Commerce
Tourism Development Office
200 North Main Street
Mount Airy, N. C. 27030
Toll Free: 1-800-948-0949
E-mail: tourism@machamber.org
Website: www.visitmayberry.com
(This website has a passel of good information.)

The Surry Arts Council
The Andy Griffith Playhouse
218 Rockford Street
Mount Airy, N. C. 27030
Toll Free: 1-800-286-6193
E-mail: surryarts@advi.net
Website: www.surryarts.org

(This website has detailed information on "Mayberry Days" as well as on other events taking place throughout the year: the Bluegrass & Old Time Fiddlers Convention, the corn-shucking event at the Living Historical Farm, the Sonka Festival, and many more.)

❖ In 1994, Mount Airy, North Carolina was chosen by The National Civic League as an All-American City. Special recognition was given for successful collaborative problem-solving, including a cross-section of citizen leaders, government, and the public and private sectors. There were 150 cities in the competition and Mount Airy was rated 36th overall.

# 37 | The Andy Griffith Show Rerun Watchers Club

THERE ARE FANS, AND THEN THERE are really loyal fans. Jim Clark of Nashville, Tennessee, qualifies for the latter category.

When *The Andy Griffith Show* went off the air in 1968, it went immediately into reruns, making the original fans of the show very happy, and touching a new generation with its wit and wisdom.

In 1979, Jim Clark was a member of an informal group at Vanderbilt University that met daily in a fraternity house to watch reruns of TAGS. Within a couple of years the group had grown considerably. Jim decided that though informal in nature, they would take the official designation of "*The Andy Griffith Show* Rerun Watchers Club," aka TAGSRWC for short. Jim said that they didn't call themselves a "fan" club, but a "watchers" club, because that's what they did, get together and watch the show.

He was aware of other informal groups meeting in his hometown of Greensboro, North Carolina and kept in touch with them. Rerun watchers groups in other areas were informally welcomed into the Club and growth was slow but steady.

Things leaped forward when, in January of 1982, Ken Beck, an editor and writer for the Nashville *Tennessean,* wrote an article for the Sunday "Showcase" section of the paper featuring Jim and *The*

*Andy Griffith Show* Rerun Watchers Club. The response was so great that Jim began putting out a newsletter, *The Bullet*, to be sent to those that had indicated an interest. The number of people desiring to start chapters of TAGSRWC was so great, it was decided that each group needed to be identified by characters from the show. The original Nashville group became the "Andy" chapter, and Greensboro signed on as "Barney."

Today, 20 years later, with nearly 1200 official chapters, the names of characters on the show were long ago used up. Most of the chapters are known by episode titles or quotations from an episode. They meet in virtually every state of the union and 8 foreign countries. Allan Newsome, the premier "Floyd" portrayer, hosts an online chapter on the internet called, "Who's Been Messing Up the Bulletin Board!" It will serve as the host for the new "e-Bullet" which will be online, replacing the printed version after all these years.

TAGSRWC members are more than just watchers these days. They have been instrumental in getting the show carried by major cable channels and continue to lobby for its airing in as many cities as possible. Also, Jim Clark has been in the forefront of promotion and assistance for Mount Airy's annual "Mayberry Days," with over 100 chapters represented at last year's festivities.

We take Goober's beanie hat off to all the dedicated folks that make up *"The Andy Griffith Show* Rerun Watchers Club," and to Jim Clark, Head Goober, for his hard work and faithful support of the show and its fans.

❖ Contact Information:

Jim Clark
TAGS Rerun Watchers Club
9 Music Square South
PMB 146
Nashville, Tennessee 37203-3286
Website: www.tagsrwc.com

"Who's Been Messing Up The Bulletin Board" Chapter
Website: www.wbmutbb.com
E-mail: floyd@mayberry.com

# I Hear Tell . . .

**EARLE** Monday and Tuesday March 23-24

Mothers Need No Longer Tell Their Daughters. Send Them to See "Enlighten Thy Daughter." It Reveals the Truth in a Gripping, Moving Drama

**Enlighten THY DAUGHTER**

A Smashing Indictment of Parental Prudery!

ALL SEATS 20 Cents
NO ONE UNDER 16 ADMITTED
ATTEND THE MATINEES

# SHOULD HUSBANDS DO HOUSE WORK?

### How Mrs. Dyer Solved the Problem.

Mrs. Mildred Dyer was lucky. She had a good-natured husband who helped her with much of her housework. Because she was in ill health for five years, it was often necessary for him to do this. But it bothered Mrs. Dyer. She felt that he had to work hard enough anyway. The time he spent in doing her work was needed for his own. She determined to find the road to better health.

She writes: "I think Lydia E. Pinkham's Vegetable Compound is simply wonderful. My health is better than it has ever been. I am getting stronger and gaining in weight."

She has solved her problem and her household is happier. The Dyers live at Redlands, Calif. Route A, Box 153.

How often does your husband have to do your housework? No matter how willing he is, no woman feels comfortable about it. Perhaps you, too, will find better health through the faithful use of Lydia E. Pinkham's Vegetable Compound.

# 38 | Mount Airy and "Mayberry" Families

## Some Family Names Existing in Mount Airy That Were Mentioned on "The Andy Griffith Show"

Allen
Beasley
Crawford
Finch
Fuller
Harris
Henderson
Hutchins
Jackson
Johnson
Jones
Leonard
Lewis
Mayberry
Myers
Nelson
Parker
Patterson
Pendleton
Phillips
Pike
Porter
Pruitt
Robertson
Rupert
Sawyer
Simmons
Simpson
Stevens
Taylor
Walker
Watson
Wilson

# 39 | *Just One More Thing*

❖ In one of the episodes, Sheriff Andy Taylor says that he took tickets and popped popcorn at the Mayberry Grand Theater when he was a youth.

  Mount Airy natives told me that Andy Griffith took tickets and popped popcorn at the Center Theater when he was in his teens.

❖ In Episode #123, "Fun Girls," as well as others of *The Andy Griffith Show,* mention was made of the Kit Kat Club, located near the county line. It served beer and was presented as kind of an unsavory place where trouble might be brewing at any time.

  In the days when Andy was growing up in Mount Airy, the Black Cat Club was a similar roadhouse, located near the Surry County/Virginia State line. There were articles in the paper almost every week about excessive drinking leading to fights.

❖ In Episode #72, "The Mayberry Band,"Sheriff Andy Taylor is shown playing a tuba in the town band.

When Andy Griffith was playing in the Grace Moravian Church band, he began playing a trombone, but also learned to play the baritone horn, B-flat alto, bass horn and valve trombone.

Each Easter Sunday morning, the Moravian Band would play celebration music to observe the resurrection of Jesus. They would start their march on South Main Street before dawn, and residents of the town would walk behind the band to the church's cemetery on North Main Street. As a young girl, I remember how exciting and uplifting it was to join the crowds following the band and be a part the special service at the cemetary.

❖ Episode #183 dealing with the Gypsies coming to town really struck a cord with me. Since I spent so much time with the policemen, and my grandfather was the Justice of the Peace, I heard them talking about the problems when the Gypsies came to town. *The Mount Airy News* even printed a warning to the citizens not to buy items from them or let them into their houses to "sharpen knives," as it might just be a ruse to steal something from them.

When I finally saw the Gypsies, I found them fascinating. The men's outfits were as colorful as the women's, and they were all olive-skinned and good-looking. (Well, to a 10-year-old girl they were!)

My mother and her friends talked about going to have their fortunes told, and Grandmother strongly warned them against it, lest they have a spell cast over them during the process.

In spite of all the warnings, many people in town did get their knives sharpened, had their fortunes told, and bought jewelry made of "gold" that rubbed off less than a week after the Gypsies had moved on.

# Related Resources

Beck, Ken, and Jim Clark. *The Andy Griffith Show Book*. New York: St. Martin's, 1985.

Beck, Ken, and Jim Clark. *Mayberry Memories:The Andy Griffith Show Photo Album*. Nashville:Rutledge Hill Press, 2000.

Bower, Neal. *Behind the Scenes of a TV Classic*. Winston-Salem, N.C.: John F. Blair, 1998.

Collins, Terry. *The Andy Griffith Story*. Mount Airy, N.C.: Explorer Press, 1995.

Harrison, Dan, and Bill Habeeb. *Inside Mayberry: The* Andy *Griffith Show Handbook*. New York: Harper Perennial, 1994.

Kelly, Richard. *The Andy Griffith Show*, 4th ed. Winston-Salem, N.C.: John F. Blair, 1984.

"The Mayberry Confidential: Official Newsletter of Mayberry Days." Published by the Surry Arts Council, 1991-2001.

Pfeiffer, Lee. *The Official Andy Griffith Show Scrapbook*. New York: Citadel, 1994.

Robertson, Jeanne Swanner. *Mayberry Humor Across the USA*. Houston, Texas: Rich Publishing Co., 1995.

Robinson, Dale, and David Fernandes. *The Definitive Andy Griffith Show Reference*. Jefferson, North Carolina: McFarland & Company, Inc. 1996

Wallace, Irving and Amy. *The Two*. New York: Simon and Schuster, 1978.

# *Index*

All *italicized* entries refer to fictional characters, events or title of an episode or television program, theatrical production or movie. All non-italicized entries refer to actual people, places, names and events.

# *Quick Order Form*

**Fax orders:** (904) 824-0145  Send this form.

**Telephone orders**: Call 1-800-540-9711 toll free.
Have your credit card ready.

**Postal mail orders**: Dynamic Living Press,
P. O. Box 3164, St. Augustine, FL 32085-3164 USA
Telephone: 904-824-9931

Please send me: *MEMORIES OF MAYBERRY, A Nostalgic Look at ANDY GRIFFITH'S Hometown, Mount Airy, North Carolina.*

Number of copies_____ @ $19.95 ea.  Total $_____

Name:_____

Address:_____

City_____State_____Zip_____

Telephone: (    )_____E-Mail:_____

**Sales tax**:  Please add 6% for books shipped to Florida addresses.

**Shipping**:  $4 for the first book and $2 for each
　　　　　　additional book

**Payment** (circle one)  Check  Credit Card:  Visa  MasterCard

**Card Number**_____Exp.Date___/___

**Name on Card**_____

**Signature**_____